My Journey
# In and Out of
# Africa

## Pauline Tusher

Stillwater Cove Press
Incline, Nevada

CATALOGING DATA:
My Journey In and Out of Africa
By Pauline Tusher

Cover and interior design: ShubinDesign.com
Cover Illustration: www.123rf.com, Panupong 1982

ISBN: 978-0-9916174-4-9

Printed in the United States of America

To my sons, Gregory and Scott,
and to their families and the generations
of their families to follow.

*All life is an experiment.*
*The more experiments you make the better.*

— Ralph Waldo Emerson

# Acknowledgments

Thank you to my husband, Tom, for encouraging me to write my story. I wouldn't be where I am without you, Tom. You light up my life.

I am also grateful to my editor, Laura Deutsch, for believing in me. Thank you Laura for your guidance, patience and some laughs along the way.

# Preface

*In and Out of Africa* tells about the forces and incidents, the perils and privileges that have come together to make me who I am—a process that continues to unfold each day that speeds by.

I suppose that all parents want their children to know their story—just as I wanted to know about my parents, and my grandchildren, Luke, Logan and Lucy, will want to know about theirs. We each look for insight into what makes us tick and often to our parents for answers to that question. But as parents, how often do we sit down and tell our story—even though it is our story that makes us each unique?

While I have shared isolated episodes in my life, this is my first attempt at telling a larger story—one that has taken me both in and out of Africa during a particularly unexpected and chaotic time in history. If my story has a message, it is that we face incredible challenges and changes in life but can survive them—in my case through determination, adaptability, luck and love.

I started writing my story back in 1991 and stopped

soon after. At the time it seemed too complicated—too many turning points and ups and downs to commit to paper. It has taken until now to finish—and still feels far from complete. Since I never kept diaries or organized archival material, my book is less an autobiography and more a personal memoir built on selected recollections and reflections.

# Introduction

One beautiful late afternoon in the spring of 1955, when I was fourteen years old, I lay on the lawn of our backyard in Moshi, a small Tanzanian town at the base of Mt. Kilimanjaro. Kili, the largest freestanding mountain in the world, was snow capped and looking very much like a Christmas pudding with the icing on top. They say that from Mt. Kilimanjaro you can see the largest expanse of the earth's surface in one sweeping view. As I lay on the lawn looking at Kili, I dreamed of one day living in the Caribbean and near the Pacific Ocean. That was just one of my dreams growing up in East Africa, where my family had moved when I was eight years old. My father had lived overseas, and I probably inherited his wanderlust.

In 1967, I married Tom, who had graduated from Stanford

Business School two years earlier. Tom became a young marketing executive working at Colgate-Palmolive in New York. A year later, we received our first international transfer to San Juan, Puerto Rico. From there we traveled to many Caribbean islands. Two years later we moved to San Francisco, where Tom was offered a job with the largest jean manufacturer in the world, Levi Strauss. It wasn't long afterwards that Tom was asked to fill in for the general manager in Mexico City, who had suffered a heart attack. I stayed in San Francisco because Tom's transfer was only for six months. At that time, I was working with Pakistan International Airlines and was able to get free tickets to join Tom on weekends. We fell in love with Mexico City—the floating markets, museums, gardens and restaurants. We even hoped that our first child would be born in Mexico, which would have allowed us to buy beachfront property there. Thirty years later—when you no longer needed to be a Mexican citizen to own land—we were able to buy property on the ocean in Baja.

In 1970, Tom was asked to open Levi Strauss in Australia. We moved to Sydney; from there, we traveled with our son Gregory, who was only a few months old, to most of the Pacific islands.

This story begins with my story of resilience and survival (along with a nice helping of luck) in my early years and continues to the present day. I arrived in Kenya in 1948 and lived in Africa until 1959, when I left for London. This was a particularly harrowing time in African history: the Mau Mau Rebellion, a bloody uprising against the ruling British colonialists in Kenya. Historical revisionism sees the Mau Mau (1952-1960) as setting the stage for a necessary Kenyan Independence, which came in 1963.

I tell the story from my own perspective, that of a frightened child of British parents, a target of Kikuyu terrorism, where the weapon of choice was a *panga*, a broad-blade machete used to carve a path through the jungle. I spent my adolescence too young to understand what was really going on around me—not that knowing more about British colonialism and the oppression of the Kikuyu people would have helped me during the terror I felt on a daily basis.

Recently, I was asked if my children knew of any of my family's near misses with the Mau Mau. They don't. Many parents raise their children in the here and now, as we did. Boys especially don't want to sit down and hear long-ago stories about their mother's African upbringing. They went to school, they had their sports activities, and they did their homework.

This book goes beyond my childhood in Africa, to my years in London and the United States and other countries around the world. I visited Africa several times after moving away. There never seemed to be time to tell my story until now.

# 1

# Born in the USA

*Birth is a beginning and death a destination.*
*But life is a journey.*
—Alvin Fine

I was born in Bronxville in Westchester County, New York, on April 17 in the year 1941. My father was Norman Paul Kensett (born August 22, 1908) and my mother, Beryl Selina Nunn (born June 4, 1914). Both Mother and Father were born in England, which gave me dual citizenship, British and American. That would later prove to be my good fortune.

Both sets of grandparents came from the borough of Ealing in West London. I never met my father's father. He drove a tram and died young, leaving my grandmother, Myrtle Kensett, alone to raise seven young boys. She had a postage-stamp garden, where she grew her own vegetables and flowers. The British love their gardens.

Grandmother lived a lonely and frugal life, filled with financial difficulty. But she was a proud woman and always impeccably dressed. When I was eighteen, and living in London, I would go visit her. She made me lemon curd tarts, mince pies, sponge cakes with raspberry jelly. I didn't know much about her but I liked her very much. I would visit Grandmother, give her some love and companionship, and talk about our family's life in East Africa.

I never learned much about my mother's family either. My grandmother, whom I called Nan, was also widowed at a young age. She sold vegetables and flowers at Covent Garden, which in those days was an enormous open-air marketplace, dating back to the thirteenth century.

Once a forty-acre walled site, Covent Garden was originally a large kitchen garden run by the Benedictine monks. In 1540, King Henry VIII dissolved all the country's monastic properties, and in the eighteenth century, as the market grew in size and popularity, it became a major destination with pubs, theatres, street entertainers, Punch and Judy shows, gas lamps, horse-driven carriages and ladies of ill repute. Today, it has a theatre, boutiques, restaurants and street entertainment.

Managing a produce stand was a difficult job for a woman in her late twenties. She had to leave home at three in the morning to get to work. When the bananas came in from abroad, Nan once told me, she would often see tarantulas. Eventually she became a milliner and started making and designing the most beautiful hats imaginable, many of them covered with colorful bird feathers. Ostrich plumes were quite the rage and very expensive, as they were imported. Today it is illegal to use these exotic bird feathers.

I loved visiting Nan on weekends. I shared her bedroom and we had tea and toast in bed in the morning and talked for hours. I made sure to wake up in time to greet the milkman in his horse-driven cart, pet the horse, and give it a carrot.

## A Bachelor's Assignment

Mummy was a teenager and Daddy in his twenties when they met and started dating. Daddy was an up-and-coming branch manager at Barclays Bank in London and Mummy was going to secretarial school and finding modeling jobs. They had been together for quite a long time when Daddy was given the chance to join the overseas branch of Barclays for an indefinite stay. It was a great opportunity and challenge for Daddy—to open up offices for Barclays in Dominica and Barbados—but it annoyed Mummy because his jobs were considered "a bachelor's assignment," which meant that she would not be going with him.

On the rebound, Mother married a wealthy Scotsman named Blakie McKim, who was fifteen years her senior.

He owned several grocery stores, which brought in a handsome income. For the first few years of their marriage, they lived in an exclusive apartment building on Pont Street near Kensington High Street in London. There, my sister, Patricia Jane, was born on October 19, 1937. Soon after Pat's birth the family bought a lovely home in the exclusive area of Gerrards Cross in Buckinghamshire.

After they moved to the new house, a dreadful snowstorm hit England, which shut the country down for three days. Pat was only two-and-a-half years old when she went out in the snow to help her father clear the driveway. She found Blakie laying face down in the snow. He had suffered a fatal heart attack. The storm was so bad that there was no telephone connection, trains weren't running, and worst of all, there was no electricity or heat. My sister and Mummy stayed in the house with Blakie's body for three days before they were able to get help.

## WWII

Like her own mother before her, Beryl found herself widowed with one small child at a young age. However, six months hadn't passed before she wrote to Norman in Barbados to tell him of Blakie's death. Blakie's family was hurt and angry that Beryl hadn't mourned for a longer period of time before contacting Norman, who proposed and asked her to sail to New York, which was his next transfer. In the end, Blakie's family came through for Mummy and Pat. Her brother-in-law in Scotland was able to pull strings and managed to secure bookings on the MS *Batory*, an ocean liner that set sail to New York from Liverpool. It was 1940 and World War II was raging.

The night before sailing, my mother, sister and grandmother, Nan, stayed at the Adelphi, a hotel in Liverpool. The following morning, they learned that Germans had bombed the city but not the hotel or the MS *Batory*. The ship was able to sail, but Mother and Pat had to wear life jackets the entire voyage, and Pat was never allowed to leave my mother's side. Mummy remembered that many of the passengers were merchant naval captains traveling to Galveston, Texas, to pick up "Liberty Ships," the WWII cargo ships made in the US and donated by the US government to help England's war effort.

Upon leaving Liverpool, the MS *Batory* traveled north of Ireland in a convoy of ships, but after three days, cruised ahead and was on its own. On the fourth day, however, passengers awoke early to what felt like the vessel jumping in and out of the ocean. Mother believed the ship had been attacked by a German submarine, although it was possible they were feeling the Batory's own deep-sea mines exploding. Whatever the cause, the effect was clear: when the passengers went to the top deck, they found masses of debris on the ship and in the ocean.

Two days later, passengers heard another frightening crash. This time when they went on top, they were in a fog bank surrounded by icebergs. When the tip of one iceberg fell on the ship's deck, the MS *Batory* remained stationary for another two days before finally limping into Halifax, Nova Scotia, for repair.

## The Little Church Around the Corner

Eventually they sailed past our wonderful Statue of Liberty and into New York, where Daddy was waiting to welcome his wife-to-be and stepdaughter. Being a banker at Barclays helped him secure a residential permit for Mummy and Pat, both British citizens, to live in New York. Soon after, Mummy and Daddy were married at the well-known Little Church Around the Corner, which still sits in neo-gothic splendor at One East 29th Street between Madison and Fifth Avenues.

I was born at the St. Lawrence Hospital in Bronxville, New York, about nine months later.

We lived in a pleasant townhouse complex in Westchester County, which backed up to a forest. I will never forget the wild bluebells and violets that grew in open space next to our home and the wonderful hot summer nights in Bronxville with endless fireflies dancing. It felt magical, as if hundreds of Tinkerbells were sprinkling down fairy dust. My father, like his mother, loved his small garden. I loved it too. I can still see the magnificent hollyhocks, long-stemmed roses and other colorful cutting flowers he grew along the side of our house.

## Memories of Bronxville

I don't remember my father being home very much. He certainly never hurried back to Bronxville after work. Instead, he would hang out with the boys and have several martinis before catching the train home where the drinking continued. I can recall the many arguments between my parents; Mother would keep his dinner hot, but he'd had too much to drink and therefore didn't want to eat dinner. Then he would fall asleep early from all the alcohol he'd consumed. Looking back, it must have been so difficult for Mummy, being in a new country, raising two daughters, and not having any support or friendship from her husband.

Nevertheless, I was a happy little girl. Once when I was very ill with the chicken pox and my mother had been gone all day, she returned with gifts to keep me occupied during the long and lonely time I spent recuperating. The days were dark as the curtains were drawn because doctors believed light would stress the patient's eyes. Mummy bought me several paper ballerinas, each two inches tall, which would swirl around when they were put in a bowl with water. They kept me happy and amused for hours. I also remember how I loved to play endlessly with paper dolls. From an early age, I could adapt to my environment. This was a good thing. I see that now.

When I was six, a friend and I were riding our bicycles. Ahead, we saw Johnny, the neighborhood troublemaker. My friend was alarmed. "He has a bow and arrow. Let's go back."

"He won't hurt us," I replied. But Johnny aimed the arrow and grazed my eye. I came home from the hospital with an eye patch; it had scratched my eye badly, but I didn't lose my sight.

When my father lived in Barbados he had found a very large and beautiful conch shell on the beach. He treasured this shell and brought it with him to the United States. On weekends when Pat and I were visiting with friends down the street, Daddy would stand outside our home at six o'clock in the evening and blow into the shell, which could be heard for a long distance. When we heard the conch, we knew we had to return home immediately as Daddy did not like tardiness. If we were not paying attention, our friends' parents would tell us the conch shell was calling us.

In 1947, our neighbors sparked excitement when they bought a television. Twice a week, we children gathered to watch a new program called "Howdy Doody," our eyes glued to the screen.

For most families, radio was the entertainment. I can still see Daddy sitting there, listening with great intent with his pipe in his mouth while my mother was darning a sock. The weekly series, such as "The Shadow Knows" and "The Green Hornet," left us in such suspense that we could hardly wait for the next episode. Our imaginations were alive; these shows were much more engaging than television is today.

## Sailing to England In 1946

As my father was on an overseas assignment, he would get home leave every two years. The first I remember was after the war in 1946 when we sailed to England on the SS *Mauritania II*, Britain's largest luxury cruise ship at the time. My parents' friends were waving banners and throwing streamers as we pulled out of the dock in New York.

So many things I recall. We sailed first-class and my parents had a luxurious cabin; the bed had a large mahogany headboard featuring two carved dolphins jumping out of the water. We were served afternoon tea while an orchestra serenaded us. I would get lost in the ship's dark-paneled library and writing room, which brimmed with beautiful desks, piles of stationery and leather-bound books. I loved everything from the comforting, warm Bovril in the morning to the lavish dinners at night. During the day, my sister and I sat in chaise lounges on the deck, wrapped in warm blankets, rolling with the rhythm of the ocean's massive waves. Everything about our two weeks at sea seemed just right. There were shuffleboard and mechanical horse racing for entertainment. From a child's point of view, it was heavenly. I imagine how wonderful it must have been for my parents—a respite from work and a time to be together.

The terrible shame was that we were living in a fantasyland, about to visit a country that had been destroyed by the Germans and their devastating bombs.

### Nan's House

We stayed with Nan, who lived in a nice little two-story house at 38 Hill Lane in the borough of Ealing in West London. I loved my grandmother, and was saddened by how her home had been damaged by the bombs, the beautiful stained-glass windows shattered. Nan was fortunate, however, that she had not lost her home—unlike many of her neighbors.

Everybody was on rationing back then. The four of us converged on poor Nan, who used her coupons for one person (for items like milk, bread, butter, meat and sugar) to feed a group of five. I never remember going hungry, but I do remember it being hard. Coal was Nan's source of heat, and that too was rationed. I dreaded going to the toilet or bathing, as the house was bitterly cold. The warmest room in the house was the living room, where we huddled around the fireplace, sometimes toasting bread with very long forks on the flames of a roaring fire. I don't quite know how Nan managed when she barely had enough for herself. It is impressive, looking back; she was obviously a very organized, terrific lady. Like the rest of the country, she had to live frugally for a long time.

My father took the family to London's financial district to see the damage that had been inflicted by the Germans. The financial district was flattened. I remember sitting on my father's shoulders as we walked through the rubble around St. Paul's Cathedral observing the destruction. It hurt me because I could feel the pain that Father was feeling as he took in the devastation. Amazingly, St. Paul's Cathedral survived the bombing.

I have great memories from the trip as well, like the clip-clop of the milkman's horse-drawn cart at six-thirty each morning. That was the highlight of my days. Then there was the scruffy Rags and Bones man, who also came with his horse and cart. How I enjoyed hearing his cry, "Rags and Bones." That was how people got rid of un-wanted household items back then.

We returned home to Bronxville on the SS *Mauritania*— and again, for two weeks, I was a pampered little girl with her big sister on a special voyage.

## 2

# A New Beginning

*Nothing can really prepare you for Africa: it is too full of
extremes and contrasts, too immense a spectrum of creation,
so much wider and more vivid than anywhere else,
that it seems to require a new set of senses.*

—Evelyn Ames, *A Glimpse of Eden*

We lived in Bronxville until 1948, when my father was
offered a job with Barclays Bank DCO (Dominion
Colonial Overseas) in Nairobi, Kenya, British East Africa.
It was a promotion for him—another overseas assignment
that, I believe, he was excited about. Of course, nothing
can really prepare you for Africa.

It seemed quite exciting to my sister and me at first,
especially when we sailed from New York to East Africa
via South Africa. Cape Town, where we stopped briefly,
left an indelible impression of a rickshaw ride that Pat

and I took with a Zulu man. It was a terrifying experience for us. To see this very tall Zulu man—with a feathered headdress full of ostrich plumes and native trinkets, with bones in his ears and nose, naked to his waist, wearing a skirt of animal skins and singing wild songs in his native tongue—was frightening for two young girls. I thought the devil had come and my life was over.

## Winding Through the Kenyan Countryside

We sailed into the beautiful Kenyan coastal town of Mombasa, which is on the Indian Ocean. Soon after we docked, we caught a train that chugged its way slowly through the Kenyan countryside; it took us more than a day to get to our final destination in Nairobi, which is 5,500 feet above sea level. I remember sitting on the steps at the end of the carriage car, the wind in my hair, holding onto the rails while admiring this magnificent East African countryside—the flat plains and shrubs as far as the eye could see, hundreds of giraffes and elephants in herds, thousands of zebras, gazelles and even more wildebeest. We had to stop and wait for a large herd of elephants to cross the tracks. This was commonplace. It was a beautiful, moving experience winding through Kenya and one that I still vividly remember. I was eight years old.

We stayed in the Norfolk Hotel in Nairobi for a brief period of time—until we were able to find housing, which wasn't easy. The British colonialists would usually work for two years in East Africa and then take a six-month home leave. This meant that you could only find housing in Kenya for six months at a time. This really was very difficult; we would move to a home, settle into a new school district, and before we knew it, it was time to move on. I associate the homes we lived in with different school uniforms. Every school I attended had a uniform, and every time we moved, it was another uniform, new friends and new teachers. It never seemed to be a real problem. Looking back, I believe this taught me to be independent. Daddy bought me a rusty third- or fourth-hand bicycle with a basket in the front, which also helped my independence. I loved riding through grass fields watching mice and snakes whip by. It gave me a sense of freedom and control over my life.

Growing up in East Africa, where there were no toy stores or bookstores, one had to make one's own entertainment. Each August Nan would ask me what I would like for Christmas, as shipping took weeks with no guarantee of arrival. It was hard to get shoes (I wore flip-flops most of the time), so that's what I always requested. I remember receiving several Dinkie cars and was entertained for hours playing in the dirt, creating freeways and bridges. I loved catching birds with a cardboard box that I had made into a trap with the lure of bread. I propped the box up on sticks, attached a string, and lay in wait until the birds came. Then I pulled the string to trap them. I caught the birds, stroked their feathers, then released them back to freedom.

My greatest gift was from a friend whose Alsatian dog had a litter, and my sister and I were given the pick of the pups. Pat chose a gorgeous, chubby little guy, and I went for one that was on the slender side. We called them Pepsi and Cola. They were both magnificent looking dogs and brought us great joy. One day a man came to our door to say he had hit one of our dogs with his car—and that was the end of poor Pepsi. Cola, on the other hand, remained my shadow, confidant and friend. He seemed closer to me and more caring than my parents ever were—or at least that's how it felt at the time.

### My Brothers are Born

My dear twin brothers Gregory and Malcolm were born in the second house we rented on the outskirts of Nairobi. On that day, March 31, 1951, Princess Elizabeth (now Queen Elizabeth) and her husband, the Duke of Edinburgh, happened to be visiting the same hospital in Kenya where Mummy gave birth to the twins. Mummy was actually holding Gregory and Malcolm in her arms when the Princess entered her room—a real thrill for Mother. It was also the same day that the Princess learned of the death of her father, King George VI, while she was staying at Treetops Lodge in the Abderdare Mountains.

Elizabeth had come to Kenya as a princess, but she left as a queen.

We had the most wonderful *ayah* (Swahili for nurse-maid) after the twins were born. Her name was Erina and she had the happiest face with bright eyes, round cheeks and perfect white teeth. We spent a lot of time talking to her in her quarters, which were in a very small concrete building behind our house. She had a bed made of sticks and rawhide, and a small table and stool. We would share her lunch (called *posho*), a bland ground maize, and dip our hands into a sauce to make it taste better. We all spoke Swahili, which Gregory and Malcolm spoke fluently even before they spoke English. I would love to track Erina down and give her a hug, and talk about those times we had together. But we were never told anyone's surname, so it would have been an impossible task to find her.

## Olduvai Gorge

Our next move was to a house we rented from the Coryndon Museum (later called the National Museum of Kenya) on the outskirts of Nairobi. The bedrooms had floor-to-ceiling filing cabinets with long, thin drawers used to store thousands of butterflies and bugs. It was a stunning collection. Our garden was on museum property. There was a large enclosed pen on the land that housed several very old giant land tortoises. I would straddle their backs and ride them, feeding them leftover cabbage and greens from our kitchen on a regular basis.

Sometimes I would ride the tortoises up to a large window of the museum and watch a man inside working on old skulls and bones. He was so intensely focused on his work that I don't believe he ever noticed me. If he did, he never acknowledged it. I found out later that the man was the renowned archeologist Dr. Louis Leakey. When I was older, I learned that in 1948, in the Olduvai Gorge in Kenya, Dr. Leakey and his wife Mary had found the ancient remains of a creature that dated back 40,000 years. Pieced together from only  thirty fragments, Dr. and Mary Leakey concluded that the creature was a common ancestor of apes and humans. I now understand why Dr. Leakey was so engrossed in his work—it must have been only a year or two after his incredible discovery.

Gregory and Malcolm were very young when we lived on the grounds of the museum. We had a 1937 Packard, which we named Stanley Steamer. It was old and constantly breaking down. I never looked forward to our outings back then, since I knew it would take forever to get to where we were going—if we arrived at all. Daddy's head was always under the bonnet of the car. Once we went to Mombasa and lost a whole day trying to get there. We were at the mercy of others, should they even stop to help.

We did see lots of wildlife roaming the bright red soil on the road to Mombasa, and we would stop for elephants crossing in front of us. There were times we had to make a quick stop to go to the "loo" in the bush. This was done nervously and quickly, since you never knew what was lurking behind you or just passing by. Once, we happened to run over a python and much to our horror, it clung to the car's running board, where it stayed for some time. No one dared to open a window or door.

From one of our houses I walked to school two miles each way through a field. I didn't enjoy this walk because I knew snakes were all around. Along the walking path there was a hedge with thorns so big that butcherbirds would catch critters in the field and impale them on the thorns. It looked like a clothesline—with rats and snakes hung out to dry. All this wildlife and potential danger was very unsettling, but at the end of each day Cola would be waiting for me, and this helped me cross the path. All I had to do was whistle very loudly several times and before I knew it, my trusted and loving Cola was jumping up on me. He was my protective bodyguard, always at my side. If Daddy raised his voice, Cola would be on the alert. Now that I had him, Daddy never dared punish me. What a comfort Cola was, especially during the Mau Mau.

# 3
# The Way of the Mau Mau

**Mau Mau**

*Mzungu Arudi Uingereza: Let the white man go home to Europe*
*Mwafrica Apate Uhuru: So the Africans can get independence*

The Mau Mau uprising had a profound impact on the way I grew up. After I left East Africa, it took me several years to get over the trauma. Tom was a great help, comforting me and giving me the love and stability that I so needed.

By the time the bloody episode was over and the Africans had gained independence—that was really what the Mau Mau Rebellion was all about—I was already an American citizen living in New York City. But at the time, I was just a young girl trying to survive my adolescence. I had no sense at all that I was living through a pivotal time in both African and British history.

It is, of course, easier in hindsight to see the whole

social and political situation in context. In the late 1800s, the British came to Kenya and took land from both the Maasai and Kikuyu people. This displaced thousands, who were forced out of their home territory to find new land for their villages and cattle. The British took some of the finest farmland in all of Kenya from the indigenous people, and over the years, the Africans got restless. They wanted their land back.

## Black and White

The British basically established a dictatorship in East Africa by keeping fundamental freedoms (such as speech, press and assembly) from "the blacks"—which is how "the whites" referred to the African people. Only whites could enjoy economic freedom, while blacks were forced into wage slavery and servitude. There were many restrictions on the Kikuyu, from how much firewood they were allowed to how much land they could own.

When we first arrived in Nairobi in 1949, we heard the whites talking about how the blacks were disgruntled with British rule and the presence of white people in general. We even heard about an underground movement called the Mau Mau. But the British, my parents included, ignored this and went on with business as usual.

If you were British or white, you were a target of the Mau Mau no matter how old you were. But it all came to a head when the Mau Mau began to terrorize their own

Kikuyu people (as well as people from other tribes) who had not turned against the whites. In 1952, the British declared a state of emergency and curfew that lasted for six years.

We heard about strange midnight Mau Mau ceremonies in the jungle that included eating human flesh and brains and drinking human blood. Then came the reports about Kikuyu people being dragged from their beds late at night—beaten and maimed and forced into taking oaths of initiation into the secret society of Mau Mau. The Mau Mau's modus operandi was obscenely bloody and brutally savage, aimed at striking paralyzing fear into the hearts and minds of all those who opposed them.

## The British Dress Code

That was the backdrop of my growing up—and under the circumstances, Mummy tried to keep life as normal as possible. One thing she did well was keep a nice home, and she was a wonderful cook.

The first home we lived in was a lovely, two-story brick house with a circular drive on Ngong Road outside of Nairobi. We had four servants. The head housekeeper, Juma, was tall and quite striking. His uniform was a white caftan with a red sash, and he wore a fez with a black tassel on the side. That was the dress code introduced by the British when they colonized India, and they brought it along when they colonized East Africa. Our servants never wore shoes.

Lunch was the big meal of the day, served to us by Juma in a formal setting. When one course was finished, Mummy would push the button under the table, which would ring in the kitchen so Juma would know to take the first-course plates away. Every week a Kikuyu *bibi* (Swalhili for "woman") would come to the house to sell us eggs or a chicken or manure for fertilizing the garden. She had walked for miles to get to us. I will never forget the first time our gardener killed a chicken. It was very upsetting to see a headless bird flapping its wings around the garden.

Our Sunday family outing was to drive out to the Ngong Hills in our small black Ford Prefect to look for elephant and buffalo dung and bring it back as fertilizer. It became a game to see who spotted the dung first. Dad would get out of the car with his pipe in his mouth, open the boot of the car, get the shovel and sack, and fill it up with precious and free manure. This made Dad happy. We would then stop for tea at the Karen Hotel—the hotel where the famous Danish writer Karen Blixen built her coffee plantation. In 1937, Blixen, under her pen name, Isak Dinesen, wrote the book *Out of Africa* about the seventeen years she lived in Kenya. Her story was later popularized by Meryl Streep, in the award-winning movie of the same name. It also featured Robert Redford in the starring role of Dennis Finch Hatton, the famous game hunter who was Blixen's lover, and who is now buried on the top of the Ngong Hills.

We had a house in Kilimani, two miles from the Kilimani School. One day we were told there was a lion on the prowl. I was worried about my brothers, who were usually alone in our garden with the ayah. I knew there was a good chance Mummy was not at home, because I often saw a man pick her up for "lunch." So, I left school in a hurry to make sure they were safe. I ran as fast as I could. But not once did I fear for myself. All was well. The lion had just passed through.

## Near Misses and the Mau Mau

I learned about fear through my introduction to the Mau Mau, with whom I had many near misses. Once, I was taking care of Daddy's vegetable garden when he was away interviewing for a job in Uganda. My mother, looking out the kitchen window, yelled, "Paulie, come here now!" She had seen a man approaching me in the garden with a panga. I could tell by the tone of her voice that this was serious. As I turned to the right I realized that the panga had been thrown exactly where I had been! Mum ran to the phone, only to find the line had been cut.

Our home in Dagoretti, west of Nairobi, had bars on all the windows. One night my father heard a ruckus and woke up to see a long pole with a hook on the end reaching through the window to his dresser. We had heard about this device before, and were advised not to grab the pole because razor blades had been inserted in the wood.

Daily life became a constant reminder of the Mau Mau. It was not uncommon to drive down a road and see dog and cat heads the Mau Mau had decapitated and staked to trees and fences. Farmers would return to their property to find beloved pets mangled, hamstrung and dead. The Mau Mau also tormented white farmers by removing their cows' udders, disemboweling their cattle or severing their tendons so they couldn't walk. When I saw the animals, it made me cry. I couldn't get the picture out of my mind. It was the Mau Mau way of saying: "You are next. We are watching you."

I had a friend, and we rode horseback together, but because of the Mau Mau Emergency we were not allowed to leave her property. After two years of the Emergency, we became bored and rode the horses through neighboring cornfields. We were cantering up a hill between rows of corn when we were suddenly charged by a group of Mau Mau with pangas. They threw their pangas but missed us. Our hearts were pounding, and we never left her property again.

### Torching Horses

Still, the reminders persisted. We moved to a remote area called Kabete where we were surrounded by coffee plantations. We lived in isolation, two miles off the main road. It was another very beautiful house, with large French doors overlooking a bucolic property with rolling hills, a running river and a forest of eucalyptus trees in the back. We used some of the fallen trees to jump when we were out horseback riding. I later discovered there were Mau Mau hideouts under those trees.

When my girlfriend went to England for six months, she asked me to take care of her three horses. I was flattered and thrilled to have them under my care. With the help of her syce, or groomsman, we built stables for them next to our house. One evening we were sitting in the living room and heard a terrible whinnying and crashing sounds coming from the horses in the stable. We knew they were in trouble and struggling. Then we saw climbing flames reflected in our French windows. My father, who was a reservist for the British Police, always wore a gun around his waist. (Mummy did too.) He jumped up and ran to the stables. The Mau Mau had thrown kerosene on the horses and torched them! I heard the gunshots as my father took each horse out of its misery. This was extremely painful for me and to explain it to my friend was even more difficult. Years later, I learned that Daddy found dead bodies in the stream on our property.

One night my father and mother went to Karen to have dinner with friends visiting from New York. I was twelve years old and the twins were two. We were left with our wonderful houseboy, Juma. I later learned that Daddy had told the police that we (my brothers and I) were on our own and asked them to patrol the house periodically. The Emergency, which lasted until 1960, put my nerves on end all of the time. Having seen the horror of those horses burned alive was almost too much. I am always amazed that my parents thought that it was okay to leave us alone with Juma. My parents must have trusted Juma with our lives; and I realize now that he must have loved our family in his way. I know he did his best to relax me by telling me stories about what it was like for him growing up. But it didn't help; I was already traumatized.

## The Ruck Family Horror

That night at eleven o'clock I saw car lights coming up our long winding driveway. I was petrified—although I reminded myself that the Mau Mau would come on foot. It was the police, and they came to tell me to wake up my brothers because we were all to spend the night at the Kabete Police station. My darling brothers were only two years old; we wrapped them in blankets and headed off to the station. The police had been tipped off that we were on a Mau Mau hit list.

In his role as a British Army reservist, my father spent many hours outside the cell of Dedan Kamathi, the man considered to be the godfather of the Mau Mau. (Later, the British Police executed him for his crimes.) That my father was sometimes his guard was never comforting to me. Was this why we had been targeted? That night at the police station, Kamathi was just a few cells down from where my brothers and I spent the night.

Thousands of Africans were brutally slaughtered during the uprising and about sixty Europeans lost their lives. But of all the atrocities against the Kikuyu people and the Europeans, none hit me harder than the gruesome murders of six-year-old Michael Ruck and his family. The savages broke into the house and killed Michael in front of his parents, then sliced open Mrs. Ruck, who was seven months pregnant, while her husband was forced to watch. Later their bodies were hacked beyond recognition. This incident brought widespread international attention to the terror that was happening in Kenya. The Rucks lived just a few miles away, where they had a farm and provided a kindergarten for their workers' children. I still wonder if they were targeted because we had been warned and then rescued that very same night. We will never know.

Living in Kabete was unsettling, especially after the Ruck murders. After that, you never knew when your own servants might turn against you as they did with the Rucks. (It was later determined that their own employees had allowed the Mau Mau in, in order to protect their own families.) When the Mau Mau demanded blood be shed, longstanding associations and friendships between blacks and whites were no longer considered of value. White people found this aspect of life particularly insidious because the only reason your servants would turn on you was if their own lives were being threatened.

We had wonderful boys—that's what we called the staff that worked for us and lived in the houses behind our own. But if the Mau Mau wanted to enter your home, they would terrorize the staff. If the staff didn't cooperate, they would murder them and their families. Thankfully, this never happened to us.

Still, I was always nervous. At night I could hear drums beating in the distance. This was frightening because it meant that Africans were communicating with each other over a long distance, like on a telephone. What were they saying? I always thought they were planning an attack on us. What was I to think? Having our neighbors so terribly murdered gave me one good reason to be scared. But what I really hated was seeing the heads of dogs, cats or cows staked to a tree. I was an animal lover and I cried for them.

While all this was happening, my father became increasingly unhappy at his job at the bank in Nairobi. He and his boss never saw eye to eye, and one day Daddy foolishly quit his job rather than ask for a transfer. In addition to his salary, he lost all the perks, the home leaves, the medical insurance—not to mention his retirement package. It was a big mistake to give up a good job without another one to go to when you had a family to care for, especially in Kenya where jobs were not available for white people. He resigned after having met a man whom he liked; the two of them decided to go into the import-export business together. But before he signed the contract, Father's future partner had a heart attack and died. Daddy had already left the bank so now he was jobless. That was unsettling for the family and, of course, for Daddy.

If you were British, you didn't just arrive in Nairobi and start looking for a job. Usually you had been transferred, like Daddy had. It's not as if there were many employment opportunities, so for him to be unemployed in Nairobi was really quite scary. After looking around, he finally was offered a job at Kilemebe, a copper mining company in the Rwenzori Mountains of Uganda, also known as the Mountains of the Moon, on the Congo border.

It was 1953. I was thirteen years old when my parents sent me to the Loreto Convent Boarding School in Nairobi, as there were no schools in Kilembe for me. The rest of the family moved to Uganda. (My sister Pat was already in boarding school in Scotland.) There was a six-month quarantine for animals to move from Kenya to Uganda, so Daddy thought it would be best to find Cola a new home, which he did. This broke my heart. Cola was my best friend and a true companion. I was more connected to Cola than anything or anyone other than my brothers. Dear friends of my parents felt my pain and gave me a gift—a pin that was a woodcarving of Cola's face. I still cherish this pin. It was beautifully made and looks just like Cola.

# 4

# Uganda, Tanganyika and Beyond

*After climbing a great hill, one only finds that there are many more hills to climb.*
—Nelson Mandela

Not being Catholic, I felt unprepared and out of place at the Loreto Convent Boarding School. It was difficult for me—services twice a day, curtseying to the nuns every time one passed by. I had to wear a navy blue tunic with a short-sleeved white blouse and a red sash around the waist. There were so many of us living in the dormitory, it was like being in an army barrack.

The day was punctuated by bells—for sleeping, classes and prayer, for sports and meals. At five o'clock in the morning we awoke to a bell and were at chapel by six. At eight in the evening, the Grand Silence began. Not a word could be spoken until breakfast the next morning.

The school was surrounded by a coffee plantation. A long row of trees led to Saint Mary's, the Catholic Boys School. My brothers, Malcolm and Gregory, were there a few years later, and they were often whipped if they didn't play by the priests' rules. Boys and girls would sneak out at night and meet in the coffee plantation. This act alone could get you expelled.

The most painful thing was parting from Cola. I thought about him constantly and missed him so badly at school that my studies suffered. One day, out of nowhere, I was sitting in biology class and looked up to see my teacher, Sister Mano, looking angrily at the door, where Cola was sniffing. He came running through the classroom and jumped on me with such joy, licking my face and whining, that he nearly knocked me off my seat. He had run away from his new home and found me at school twelve miles away. Needless to say, I was shocked to see him and ecstatic—I began sobbing and kissing my sweet dog. Sister Mano (Swahili for "teeth," which was ironic because she never smiled, but had very large white teeth) was furious that a dog had interrupted her class. As she approached my desk, I heard the swish of her starched white habit, her rosary swinging from right to left, and the click of her shoes on the highly polished tiled floor. Her arms flying in different directions, she yelled at him to get out.

The headmistress called Cola's new family, who came and took him away from me. I was heartbroken a second time. They then had to put him on a leash and chain him up so he wouldn't escape to return to me. My dear friend Cola had never been to the convent, yet he had tracked me down to be at my side. What a special bond we had, but that was the last time I saw Cola.

## The Wild Ride Home

To get to Uganda to visit my family was a real journey. I caught a train from Nairobi to Kampala, the capitol of Uganda. We stopped at dozens of stations along the way. It was so noisy at night, with Africans begging at the stations, holding their small children, and the sounds of the goats, chickens and donkeys that were on the platform. Someone was always trying to sell beads or baskets to the travelers on the train. Their hands stretched out for shillings.

It broke my heart to see so much poverty. I will always remember the toddlers—the flies swarming in their eyes, on their faces, up their noses, their tummies swollen from malnutrition. The children were naked, or if they were lucky, they had a small torn shirt, but no shoes. So many dogs were homeless and starving and looking for scraps. The donkeys and horses also suffered from starvation. Were I able to have my own way, I would have brought them all home with me.

Once we arrived in Uganda, I had many hours of traveling by jeep over dusty, washboard dirt roads. The next step was a fixed-wing plane, which was the highlight of the trip and worth my long journey home. Just as we arrived at the airstrip, a large grass landing strip with a tiny mud hut at the end, we had to circle several times to get the hundreds of elephants, buffalo or zebras to move so we could land. It was exhilarating.

## Quiet Giants

Finally, another Land Rover would take me home to Kilemebe Mine, which was high in the Rwenzori Mountains. The vegetation was so dense where we lived, we were not able to see the open plains. We weren't too far from silverback gorillas, which we visited but could only see at a distance. When visiting the gorillas, we saw many magnificent black-and-white colobus monkeys jumping from tree to tree. They seemed to be flying. Unfortunately, deforestation has wiped out their habitat, and hunters are after their fur and meat. It was also Pigmy, or little people, territory. I remember they were very shy.

We lived modestly in a small house where the electricity was run by a generator. Our "loo" was outdoors and we weren't allowed to use it at night due to the leopards and lions in our immediate area. At night, Daddy would say, "Okay, all lights out," which meant we had to jump into bed. There was a rope from our generator into the master bedroom. Once we were tucked in, Daddy would pull the rope and all lights went out very slowly. If we needed the toilet, we had a potty under our bed.

We were in earthquake country and would wake up many times during the night to find our beds had inched their way into the middle of the room. We would watch the dresser swaying back and forth and hope it wouldn't fall on us.

My father was a keen gardener and grew all of our vegetables and flowers. One morning, I woke up to hear Daddy say, "Those bloody elephants have been in our garden again." They were such quiet giants, you never heard them passing through. It was disheartening to see our vegetable garden, which we'd put so much time into, eaten and flattened by a herd of elephants.

One time, when I was home, I remember Mum and Dad were waiting for my school report. I was nervous, because I knew it would only be bad news. I would go to the post office when I knew the mail had been delivered. I did this for a few days, until it finally arrived. I immediately tore up the letter and flushed it down the toilet. I don't think they ever followed up with the school; they never asked me about it.

My parents weren't happy in Uganda. It was a copper mining town and there was very little socializing, which my mother loved and missed. Daddy was offered a job in Moshi, Tanganyika (Tanzania today), as manager of the Tanganyika Coffee Curing Company. That was another move. Moshi had a very small population—perhaps only 2,000 Europeans, and many Asians and Africans.

## Switchboard Operators

We had very little money, so I was able to talk my father out of the expense of sending me to another school—and he agreed we needed the extra income. I was only fourteen years old and in retrospect I am sorry I didn't continue my education, but at the time I was happy to be out of school. I wasn't cut out for a convent. Instead, I got a fun job as a telephone operator at the Moshi telephone exchange with my good friend Annabel Pegg.

That was back in the days of telecommunications when people, usually women, manually connected phone calls at a switchboard. There were eight of us who worked at the exchange, which was housed in downtown Moshi. All calls made from Moshi were routed through us. We would say, "Number, please," and connect people to their local and overseas calls. Moshi was so small we got to know the people making the calls, and it became quite personal. A lot of people called me by my first name: "Hello, Paulie. Please connect me to...." There were party lines for people in the country and each home had its own ring—two, three or four times to personalize it. However, as there wasn't much to do in the evenings, people would listen in on their neighbors' calls, as we did.

On weekends, there was very little activity, so Annabel and I were able to connect everybody's telephone calls and still find time to listen in on various phone conversations, usually the ones we knew would be private and flirtatious. Needless to say, this was strictly verboten. But we were fourteen and full of mischief. There was a young Greek man we knew who owned a deli. We also knew he was attracted to a receptionist at the Kilimanjaro Hotel. Annabel and I liked to ring the Greek and then the girl at the hotel at the same time—and presto, they were talking to each other. It took them a while to figure out that they were being connected without ever placing a call. Meanwhile, Annabel and I were in stitches. Finally, they realized we were up to no good. We picked the right couple to play with: Eventually, the two got married.

To make more money I would work in the coffee plantations with the Africans picking coffee beans. I was the only white girl, and it was a backbreaking job for the time and the pay. It took forever to fill a kerosene can with coffee beans and we earned two shillings a can.

### The Vespa Virgins

Annabel and I both saved up some money and bought Vespas, which was wonderful. It gave us our freedom. We were able to get to work and we would travel for miles exploring the area.

It was 1957 and stiff petticoats were all the rage. We would wear three of them at a time with colorful trim at the hems. To ensure extra stiffness, I starched them in a bathtub for several hours. I would dry my petticoats standing up in a colorful row on the lawn. When we rode the Vespas, our skirts would blow and you could see our petticoats.

My license plate was MS4412 and Annabel's was MS4411. We were known as the Vespa Virgins. I would take Malcie and Gregory on the back of my Vespa for outings. We liked to visit the Kibo Hotel at Marangu on the slopes of Kilimanjaro. When we got there (which took several hours), we would sit on an enormous boulder in the nearby river. A waterfall cascaded behind us and we enjoyed the rushing water, which was melted snow from the mountain. We would also drive to Arusha, over seventy-five miles of dirt road from Moshi. We saw herds of impalas, zebras, and giraffes on the plains during our trips.

We had a nice home on the edge of the Karanga River, about eight miles from Moshi in a place called Shantytown that looked up at Mt. Kilimanjaro. It wasn't shabby even then, but today it's an expensive neighborhood. My brothers would go sleuthing and come home with rhino skulls and other animal carcasses. They also found snake eggs the size of chicken eggs, but transparent. If you moved the egg, you could see the embryo floating inside. "Look, Paulie," they would say when they brought snake eggs up to my face.

We always slept under a mosquito net. It was a good thing too, because once I saw a tarantula sitting on the net and it practically paralyzed me with fear. It was not unusual to have snakes under the bed, which was why we always looked down before our feet ever hit the ground. The twins would come into my room in the morning and wake me up by lifting the net and shoving a chameleon-on-a-stick in my face. I don't know why they found this behavior so terribly funny, but they roared with laughter each time. I was scared to death as I thought it would fall off the stick onto my face. To this day, I'm afraid of lizards and my brothers are probably the reason for this.

## Troubled Times

Moshi always brings back sad memories. Water was scarce and at times only mud would come through the faucet. To take a bath, we would turn on the water and let the mud settle so we could find some water—always murky with bugs floating on top. Often, only mud dripped from the faucet, so to have our bath we had to stand in mud and scoop up the water that would come to the surface. Hence, we bathed quickly and were no cleaner afterwards.

Money was in short supply, and several times Daddy couldn't pay for the electricity or water bill and was nearly taken to jail. Fortunately my sister, Pat, who was married by then, and my brother-in-law Jack frequently bailed my parents out.

I can still see Jack, who was originally from Glasgow, in his dashing British Police uniform: starched khaki shorts, khaki shirt with brass buttons and epaulets, a whistle attached to a lanyard, a wide shiny black leather belt with a gun on the right side, knee-high khaki socks with highly polished black lace-up shoes, and a policeman's hat with a shiny black brim.

Pat had inherited money when her father died, which enabled them to live the social life they both loved, and to help when Daddy had financial problems (which was all the time). They had two daughters, Linda and Jacqueline.

Mummy and Daddy were not getting on and were both drinking. The drinking had been going on for many years, but with the hardships it seemed to get worse.

I had left my job at the telephone exchange by this point and got another one as a receptionist for an accounting firm working for Larry Steele, the nicest man. One day I was not feeling well and left work around one o'clock. When I got home, a Land Rover was waiting in the drive and I saw Mother walking out the door with a suitcase. And that was it. She was leaving us. She didn't say anything to me, except to ask why I was home early. Jumping into the Land Rover, she slammed the door and the driver pulled out. She never looked back at me, or said goodbye to me or the twins. I was in shock, but I kept thinking that she would return in a few days. Instead, she abandoned us.

Before I knew it, I was raising a family and trying to comfort my brothers and Father. I was fourteen and it was now up to me to step in and take care of the family, get the twins to school, and arrange meals and house-keeping with our four houseboys. I felt like little Miss Atlas, when I was really the one who needed to be held up.

There was a wonderful natural pool in Moshi where my friends and I would swim. Eric (Mummy's boyfriend) must have known about this pool because he would show up there and try to get my attention. I really disliked the man. I felt self-conscious in a bathing suit because I was slow in developing, so I bought a pair of falsies made of rubber. I will never forget diving into the pool thinking I was so cool. But the falsies popped out of my costume, only to float on top of the water. Of course the guys (Eric included) thought the whole incident was hilarious, and I was mortified. It is not hard to imagine how I was later humilated to learn that Mummy was going out with this dreadful man who had shown interest in me.

## Uncle Harold

Daddy was drinking his money away and Mummy had taken up with Eric, an electrical engineer. I called him the Lounge Lizard. Eric and Mummy moved into the Ridgeway Hotel about three miles from our house. I would take the boys to school on the back of my Vespa and there were times when I would see Mum and Eric leaving the hotel in his red truck. The boys kept saying, "Paulie, what is Mummy doing there? When is she coming home?" I never had an answer. Then a few weeks later, she and Eric moved to Tanga, which was several hundred miles away.

Daddy's brother, Uncle Harold, was living in Lagos, Nigeria, and contacted Daddy to say he would love to come visit us in Moshi. Dad was excited, but also nervous since Mummy, or Beryl as they both called her, was no longer with us. Daddy didn't want Harold to know that he and Mummy were not together, so he tracked Mummy down and insisted she come for lunch.

Daddy told me to put a nice lunch together, but he never told me that Mother would be joining us. I had arranged with the *pichi* (cook) to prepare roast beef, Yorkshire pudding and gravy, canned peas and carrots. Dessert was canned fruit salad with whipped cream. I came home from work after picking up the twins, excited to see Uncle Harold. To my utter amazement, Mummy greeted us as if she had never left. Daddy had tracked her down in Tanga and begged her to come home for a visit. I was speechless. When Harold left after a very strained luncheon, my mother was angry with me and shouted, "Are you only eating canned food?" I burst into tears. I had really tried so hard to put on a nice lunch and I had succeeded. She left again—this time for several years.

Soon after, Uncle Harold asked if I would like to go with him to Mombasa, which was a fabulous holiday spot on the Indian Ocean. I was so ready to get away and be with my long-lost uncle. We checked into a lovely hotel overlooking the Indian Ocean. The view couldn't have been more glorious. We were right on the beach, which was miles and miles of soft, white, powdery sand, framed by palms, with dhows—traditional Arab sailing vessels, used to voyage from Arabia to the Persian Gulf, Red Sea and Indian Ocean—sailing by. Centuries ago in Zanzibar, off the Tanzanian Coast, Arab merchants traded their porcelain, glass beads, gold, carpets and palm oil for slaves, cloves, ebony and ivory.

Uncle Harold and I had separate rooms, but it soon dawned on me that that was not what my uncle had in mind. I panicked and returned to Moshi. I never saw him again and later learned that he died in Lagos of malaria.

When Daddy got behind on the rent at the Moshi home, we had to leave. He found another home down the street, and I arranged for our houseboy to help me do the packing and moving into our new home. The first night in our new place (also in Shantytown), the twins and I were unable to sleep because the mattresses were living nests of bedbugs. The little critters were climbing all over us and we were a mess with sores all over our bodies. The houseboys spent several days sterilizing the mattresses and airing out the house for us. I have no idea where Daddy was during this transition.

## Dancing with Costa

I was fortunate to have made wonderful friendships with three Greek families in Moshi. They were my rock, my saviors. My boyfriend, Costa, and his best friends, Nic and Sylvie Emmanuel, and I became very close. Like me, Sylvie was English, which created a tight bond between us. Nic's brother, also named Costa, was married to Ketty. They also became my good friends.

I loved my boyfriend a lot, and I believe he loved me, but his family didn't like the idea that I was an English girl and came from a broken home. Although they never liked me, we continued to date and spend as much time as we could at the homes of his friends.

Costa and I would go together to the Greek Club when they had social gatherings. I was struck that so many women were dressed in black. To me it seemed very depressing, but they were widows and the Greek Club was their one big outing. The older people sat around the room and when the younger people got up to dance, their eyes were always on Costa and me. Like clockwork, every time we danced, his mother got a migraine headache, and he would have to leave early to take his parents home.

Some evenings Costa and I would gather with the Emmanuel brothers and their wives for a lovely dinner and several glasses of sherry. We'd look at slides of our safaris and relive the fun we all had. We often went on safari with our own equipment and camped out at night, listening to the distant howling of the hyenas and the roaring of lions. Nothing is ever still at night in Africa, with so many animals communicating with each other in different ways. One time we killed a zebra, which was meat for the African boys who came with us to set up camp and cook dinner. We hung the zebra on a nearby tree, which attracted lions and hyenas. The safaris with these dear friends were very special times for me—watching the sunset, drinking wine and chatting at the campfire as we listened to the surrounding wildlife in the bush.

Sometimes we went to the coastal town of Pangani for a holiday and stayed in a *rondavel*, a traditional, circular African dwelling with a thatched roof. We would throw nets into the Indian Ocean and catch hundreds of sardines that we brought in and barbecued. So quickly we ate them, usually with a little lemon juice on top. These simple meals were delicious, and I have fond memories of those times.

Costa was a wonderful man and helped keep me together. I think I cared for him so much because he represented the love and security I no longer had in my home life. But even rock-solid friendships cannot mitigate the sorrow of an unhappy home life.

### Exotic Forays

The British colonialists enjoyed being in the rugged bush and created the first romantic images of a "safari," which means journey in Swahili. With their canvas tents, hurricane lanterns and rituals of tea and cocktails, they made exotic forays into the wild actually look civilized. The safaris produced in Hollywood movies were even more exotic. We were pretty basic, but we had camp beds and big kerosene lanterns. The boys would bring us tea first thing in the morning. We had a barbecue for dinner and sat on folding chairs at a big table. The bush was our loo. We hoped there were no snakes or lions lurking.

## 5

# Time to Say Goodbye

*Remember when life's path is steep*
*to keep your mind even.*

—Horace

When I was coming up on eighteen, I felt like I was on the verge of a nervous breakdown. The twins were eight and I really believed that if I moved to London, Mummy would return to take care of them. I knew while I was watching over them, she had no reason to come back.

When I told my father I was moving to London, he was against it. Dad said I could not leave until I was nineteen. I had been saving for this trip, but money was still my problem. The only thing I had to sell was my Vespa. Dear Nic came to my rescue and gave me fifty pounds for it— a very generous price. I asked Nic what he was going to do with the scooter and he told me it was just what he needed to get around his *shamba* (estate). I thanked him. Forty years later when I went to Moshi to thank him again, I learned that I had not provided the papers he needed to take it anywhere beyond his estate! Thank you Nic, for helping me during a time of need.

I wrote to my mother's brother, Uncle Eric, in Wembley, a borough of London, mentioning that I wanted to live in London, and asking if he had any suggestions for where I might get a job. He knew the general manager of the Cumberland Hotel at Marble Arch, who offered me a job as a receptionist. It was perfect, as it came with a small room and meals.

Costa drove me to Nairobi for my flight to London. I was only eighteen years old.

Just as I thought, Mummy returned to Moshi and later moved with the twins and Eric to Arusha. As hard as it was, and as much as I loved the twins and my friends, I knew I was doing the right thing by leaving Africa and starting anew. I would have had no future had I stayed.

# 6
# Lambeth Bridge

*Life breaks us all, but in the end we are stronger*
*in the broken places.*

—Ernest Hemingway

My flight to London went via Cairo and Beirut. I saw the Pyramids Sound and Light Show in Cairo beneath a starry sky—it was stunning and unforgettable. As dusk fell we arrived at the base of the pyramids; the sun set and the moon rose over the 440-foot sphinx. Laser-beam lights of pink, yellow and blue washed over the pyramids, while a narrator told us the story of the ancient pharaoh's life and death.

I loved the chaos and the colors of the Arab bazaars, where I had time to browse. Driving through the countryside was like being in biblical times, with ox-drawn carts and people going to the Nile River with containers for their water. In Beirut, once considered the Paris of the Middle East, I had a wonderful visit with the Carrs, my friends from Moshi who had been transferred there.

When I arrived in London, I was shocked to see white people unloading cargo, sweeping the streets and doing the manual work. While I was disturbed by my reaction, I understood it. I had grown up in Colonial East Africa, the child of parents who kept each race in its place, and was accustomed to seeing only Africans doing this kind of work.

That was not my only upset. Soon after landing in London, I received a letter from my mother saying that Daddy was abusing her and that they were in desperate need of money. I, too, was hurting financially, but with Mummy giving me the sad story about how hard things were, I started to worry about them. I sent them the fifty pounds that I had saved to start my new life in London. It was a huge amount of money for me, money I needed.

## A Close Family

When I first arrived and felt lonely, I would spend the weekends with my mother's brother (Uncle Eric), his wife (Aunty May) and my cousins (Susan and Carol). May and Eric had a long and loving relationship. I was often emotional when I saw the touching little things they did together, like holding hands on the couch when they watched TV. I had never seen such a thing as a good marriage in my family. Once I was settled in London, Uncle Eric would visit me. When he left, he would slip me ten pounds, a true gift that helped me through the upcoming week.

I left the Cumberland and took a job at the National Hunt and Jockey Club at Cavendish Square, where I was in charge of registering jockey colors. Each jockey who raced had his own colors and design, which changed with each horse the jockey rode. This was an overwhelming job, because there were already hundreds of thousands of different design and color combinations, and I couldn't afford to make a mistake by repeating one. Today it is computerized. The royal family's Ascot Races alone could have kept me busy. The Queen's emissary was helpful, because he already knew what jockey colors he wanted. Once, Gregory Peck came in to register his jockey's colors. What a charming man!

After three years in London, I had the travel bug and felt adventurous. I was restless, looking for another country to move to. At the time, I was living with five girls in a flat at 38 Elm Street off of Kings Road in Chelsea. One roommate was South African, two were English and two were from East Africa, like me. Francis, my East

African roommate, and I had talked to an employment agency about opportunities overseas, and before we knew it, we had an interview lined up with a wealthy Iranian man who was looking for two nannies for his family. Francis and I thought that this would be a great chance for us to live and work in a culture we knew nothing about.

## "Put On The Brakes"

The Iranian invited us to his luxurious suite at the elegant Dorchester Hotel on Park Lane in London, where we had tea and talked about the job and what our responsibilities would be with his family. He was very intelligent, his manners were perfect, and he was well spoken and impeccably dressed. He offered us the job, which included living with his family, and wanted us to start within the next five to ten days. He asked for our passports so he could immediately obtain our work visas. I didn't like the short notice and felt uncomfortable giving my passport to a stranger. It all seemed too soon for me; I had an apartment lease in Chelsea and a job where I had to give two weeks notice. I became nervous because of the pressure he put us under. Something didn't feel right. I called Uncle Eric and told him that while I was excited about a job offer as a nanny in Iran, I felt uncomfortable about starting immediately and having to break my contracts.

My uncle was also concerned and told me, "Put on the brakes." He called the MI5 (British Military Intelligence) to check out the situation. We found out that this was a scheme to get young foreigners with no ties in England to go to Iran and become "white slaves." We would have been sent into the mountains to become prostitutes to whomever. Our families would never have been able to find out where we were or whether we were even alive. Uncle Eric explained this to me. I was so relieved and happy that I had listened to my instincts and talked to him before handing over my passport. Unfortunately, this is not an unusual story. I was blessed to have been saved from such a terrible fate. Had I not followed my instincts, I would not be writing this today.

All told, I spent four years in London trying to make ends meet. It was very hard. After living in Chelsea, I moved to Swiss Cottage, a district of north London, into a very large Victorian with several roommates. We paid for heat by putting shillings (of which I didn't have a lot) in the meter. In the winter it was so cold, the frost was on the inside of the windows and wouldn't melt until late morning. I would sleep late on the weekends to avoid the discomfort of leaving my warm bed. I was earning ten pounds, ten shillings a week. I had to pay for transportation, food, clothing, and the odd movie or theatre ticket if I was lucky. I was also going to secretarial school. Meanwhile, I had several letters from my mother telling me how difficult things were at home and how badly they needed money. She always promised to pay me back, which she never did.

I got to a point where I couldn't take it any more. Mother was constantly telling me about family problems. This took its toll and I seriously thought about taking my life. I remember walking on the Lambeth Bridge, standing there and actually thinking about jumping. I then pulled myself together and said, "Paulie, there is a great life ahead of you."

During that adversity, I made one of the best decisions of my life and that was to move to New York. I had dual citizenship. How lucky was I?

*Pauline at the Outspan Hotel*
*in Aberdare National Park, Kenya, 1958*

*Tom and Pauline's wedding
Berkeley, January 1, 1967*

*Erina,
Malcolm (left),
Gregory (right)*

*Nairobi, 1951*

*Gregory, Scott and Pauline   Kenya, 1983*

*Scott and Gregory   Kenya, 1983*

Tom,
Gregory,
Scott
and Pauline

Equator in Kenya,
1983

Virginia and Gregory with children Logan, Lucy and Luke.
Sun Valley, Idaho, 2011

Scott and Christine

South Africa,
2013

Pauline and
Malcolm

Tanzania,
2011

Pauline, Nic and Sylvie Emmanuel   Tanzania,  2011

*Tom and Pauline   Blanket Bay, New Zealand  2007*

*Pauline and Billy*

*Blanket Bay*
*New Zealand*
*2007*

7

# New York, New York

*Yearning to breathe free.*

—Emma Lazarus

She was towering over us, with a torch that seemed to scrape the sky in her hand. The pale green Statue of Liberty rose above the blue water on an enormous pedestal, her arm uplifted like an Olympian carrying the flame. As we sailed by the New York skyline, I was on deck and started crying. This was truly a dream come true for me, a young girl starting a new life with one metal trunk and $100 in her purse.

When I decided to move to America in 1963, it was during the "brain drain," a time when physicians, scientists and businessmen from post-war Europe competed for work visas in the United States and Canada. Finally, being the daughter of British parents and born in New York state gave me an advantage over other people in England.

I had arrived in the UK on my British passport, but had to surrender it at the American Embassy in Grosvenor Square in order to obtain my US passport. I stood in line for two days from eight o'clock in the morning until five in the evening to be registered. A small price to pay! I didn't even like London and was anxious to start a new life in the United States.

Like many of my journeys, coming to America was quite tricky. I could only afford a cargo ship, which sailed from Bristol. Unlike passenger ships, which sail at a certain time and place, cargo ships keep changing and canceling the departure until all of the cargo has arrived. They were notoriously unreliable. It was frustrating and frightening, as I had given notice at work and was eating away at the money I would need in New York. Eventually, the ship sailed; I was the only woman on board. It took twenty-one days of high seas, waves at fifteen feet, the decks permeated with the stench of oil from the heavy machinery. We made one stop in Halifax, Nova Scotia, before arriving in New York.

### A Change Of Plans

At the end of the trip, the captain paged me on the intercom. He told me about a change in plans; we were originally supposed to dock in New York Harbor, but we were going to New Jersey instead. This really worried me: How I was going to get into Manhattan? The captain told me to take a taxi, which would cost me around forty dollars. I only had a hundred dollars to take care of myself until I was able to find a job. I panicked, but there was nothing I could do. I had come this far and there was no turning back.

Once we pulled into the dock in New Jersey, I was called, once again, to the captain's office. This time he told me there was a limousine waiting to take me to New York. I thought they had the wrong person, but the driver gave me a letter from a woman named Edie Radley. She was a friend of Tania Carr, who had lived in Moshi and grown up on the Enduimet Estate on the slopes of Kilimanjaro.

Tania had introduced me to Edie in London and we had become quite close. I told Edie that it was a big step for me to move to New York, but that I was excited. She asked when I was arriving, but there was no arrival date because I was coming by cargo ship. We said goodbye and looked forward to seeing each other in the City at some time in the future.

### "Stay As Long As You Like"

The driver of the limo gave me a letter from Edie welcoming me to New York. Edie had tracked down which ship I was on and followed its schedule to New

Jersey. She wanted to help me and generously offered to let me stay with her in her New York flat for as long as I needed. When I arrived at her lovely apartment, there was a note saying, "Please make yourself at home. Help yourself to anything in the refrigerator and stay as long as you like."

I was in shock, really, trying to understand how this incredible act of kindness could possibly be happening to me. At the same time I was overwhelmed by her gesture. I reached out to the chauffeur to give him a tip, but he wouldn't take it. Edie had taken care of that too. Someone was looking down on me and guiding me. Thank you, dear Edie, for the remarkable start to my new life.

After staying with Edie for a week, I felt I had to find a place to live. I couldn't go on using her hospitality. I found the YWCA, which was a very nice building on East 72nd Street. I had a small bedroom, very small, but it was mine. We dined cafeteria style, and there was a large lounge where we socialized. I made some good friends there. A lot of us loved the rooftop, where we would wear bikinis, cover ourselves in baby oil, and bake. Those were the days when you wanted to be brown. This is coming back to haunt me now, with skin cancers that have to be removed, but we were young and no one knew then about the dangers of the sun. Then I met Phyllis, and we shared a flat at 435 East 79th Street. We had a lot of fun together.

I went down several roads looking for a job. I considered becoming a social worker, but my visits with a social worker to impoverished homes and to the trauma center and children's wing at Bellevue Hospital were too disturbing. Battered children in plaster-of-Paris casts, their arms and legs stretched out, children covered in cigarette burns. I quickly realized I had my own problems and there was no way I had the strength to give advice to these broken families when I also came from one.

Instead, I pursued my dream job (which was apparently everyone else's as well): working for *McCall's* magazine or *Ladies' Home Journal*. Their opulent offices in Rockefeller Center overwhelmed me—a 23-year-old from East Africa, with no education—applying to coveted magazines where people with degrees in journalism and bachelor's and master's degrees were looking for jobs. I was so nervous filling out the application forms that my writing was shockingly poor. I fudged my education, as I hoped they would not be checking it in Kenya. All I was hoping for was a job as a receptionist.

Even that did not happen, which was no surprise to me, but a disappointment nonetheless. I really wanted that dream job with a magazine. But then I found a job as a receptionist with Burson-Marsteller, the public relations agency. This was my first job in New York. I was lucky because I really enjoyed the people I worked for there. However, the job itself did not suit me and I knew this was not what I wanted to continue doing. At the same time I was becoming homesick for East Africa and missing my brothers. I knew I would never be able to save enough money to pay for my airfare to return, so I decided to seek employment with an airline, which would enable me to get free or discounted tickets.

First I tried Pan Am, but to no avail. Then around that time, I met someone who helped me. I was invited to have dinner with friends of my parents in Manhattan. I happened to mention that working for Pan Am was my greatest wish, but I couldn't get in the door. This kind man who knew Mother and Father arranged for me to interview with the manager of sales. After taking tests and passing them, I was offered a job in telephone sales booking reservations. I was given the late shift—from 3:00 P.M. to midnight—but later was promoted to work at the ticket counter at 550 Fifth Avenue.

I loved this job. I was face-to-face with people and helping them with their vacation or business travel plans. I will never forget all the Jamaican people who wanted to return home—and pay with cash. Once, the airfare dropped to $155 round trip for ten days and there was a rush on the ticket counter. The Jamaican women did not carry purses. Rather, they hid their money in their underwear. To pay, they would put their hands down their blouses or up their skirts and pull out cash and coins. This was before we had hand sanitizers! A lot of people would pay with a collection of nickels and dimes, their life savings, which they'd hidden under their mattresses. I would have to sit and count coins as the line got longer and longer and people grew more and more agitated.

My next position was as a customer service agent for Pan Am's brand new helicopter shuttle that went from the top floor of the Pan American Building (now known as the MetLife Building) to JFK Airport and back again. This was an expensive service, but for those who could afford it, it cut out the traffic jams and other concerns about getting to the airport on time. I greeted guests and read the wind velocity to make sure it was safe for the helicopter to take off. I flew once, and I must say that when the helicopter lifted off and then reversed itself before going forward, I found it frightening, looking down from the 60th floor where there was nothing but a void! When six people were killed in a helicopter accident in 1977, the helicopter service was stopped, never to operate again. After my stint with the helicopter, Pan Am created a travel desk for African safaris. My background was perfect for this, and they asked me to run it.

### Cadillac Convertible

I met a young man named Richard, a Southerner, and we dated briefly. He invited me to visit his wealthy family in Palm Beach for Easter. They had a large estate near the Breakers Hotel and he offered to pay my airfare. I insisted on paying my own way, and because I couldn't afford the airfare I took a Greyhound bus instead. It was boring and endless, as we stopped at bus stations along the way.

Richard's mother was not impressed that her son was dating a girl who commuted by Greyhound. I was speechless when we passed through the gates and drove down the long driveway lined with royal palms. Servants stood by as we entered the foyer with its sweeping staircase. I admired the gorgeous house filled with beautiful art and antiques—and immediately I knew it was going to be a weekend where I needed some very elegant clothes, which I didn't have.

Before leaving, I had gone to Gimbels department store on 34th Street and bought a spinach-green polyester dress to wear, not knowing we were going to the posh family country club for Easter dinner.

I felt so uncomfortable and out of place. When it was time for dinner, my spinach-green dress and I walked down the staircase. It seemed like a nightmare. Richard's mother, beautifully dressed with magnificent jewelry, was looking up at me from down below. But she was clearly looking down on me. I knew then I was not what she wanted for her son.

We spent the day at the stuffy Bath and Tennis Club, no Jews, no coloreds allowed. I was not in my element. I couldn't wait to get back to my very small room in New York where I could breathe again. When it was time to leave Palm Beach, Richard again offered to pick up my airfare. This time, I was most grateful.

Richard and I continued to see each other. I had told him how much I loved Cadillac convertibles because they were something you didn't see in Tanzania. About a week later, the doorman called and said, "Miss Kensett, there is a gift for you downstairs." I gasped when I saw the brand-new baby blue Cadillac convertible outside my entrance. I was speechless. Instead of being happy, I was so mad at Richard and all his presumptions that I ended our friendship immediately. Here he was, raised with everything. I was raised with nothing and the idea of this extravagance was too much for me.

Being a single girl in New York was exhilarating at times and at other times very lonely. Plus, living on a very tight budget didn't help. I did meet some appealing men, including David, who worked for Chubb and Co. We would visit his family in Rhode Island quite often on weekends. I became attached to them—his sister, parents, aunts and uncles with whom we spent Christmas.

David and I dated for two years. However, I needed to know where this friendship was going. We arranged to have dinner at a lovely restaurant at the top of an apartment building on 82nd Street, overlooking the East River, to discuss our relationship. I bought a pretty black dress and felt attractive. We had a martini or two and a lovely dinner. But the evening ended when David told me the relationship was ending. This was a blow to my ego and heart. I felt very sad; we'd had such fun together and not seeing his family was going to be hard. I did stay in touch with them for several years. Looking back, that breakup was the best thing that happened to me. I was so happy that I had initiated the discussion. Had I not, it would have gone on longer and I would have never met dear Tom.

## Limuru

I was very homesick, missed my brothers, and was anxious about their well-being. I was thrilled to get my fifty-percent discounted tickets, which enabled me to fly to Nairobi. It had been eight years since I had seen the family.

Mummy, who had left my father in Tanzania, was living with Eric in Limuru in the highlands, a beautiful, albeit isolated area with many coffee plantations. Soon after I arrived, they left me alone with their dog Muffy, a white miniature poodle, and went to pick up Gregory and Malcolm from the airport. To this day, I don't know why they left me at home alone. I was a nervous wreck. It was dusk. Muffy picked up on my negative energy and started trembling.

By then the British had crushed the Mau Mau Rebellion, but historians consider the rebellion a key element to Kenyan independence, which finally came in 1963.

When I visited in 1965, the Mau Mau were still very much in the minds of Europeans. In the eleven years of the Mau Mau's murderous movement, 5,000 Mau Mau rebels and 13,000 African civilians had died, but it showed the British (and the rest of the world) that the Africans were not going to accept white minority rule. Ultimately, the British gave the Kenyans their money and their land back.

Alone in my mother's home, I was still terrified. The phone rang and I answered it, expecting to hear from my boyfriend in New York, but no one was on the other end. The phone rang again. Still, there was no one on the other end. This kept happening. I thought immediately the Mau Mau were after us and were coming to our home, which was in a remote area and had French doors and windows. I felt they could look in and see where I was in the house. My paranoia of the Mau Mau got to me and I felt as if I had a thousand eyes watching my every move. Muffy and I hid behind the living room curtains and sat on the floor and cuddled together for a few hours with our hearts pounding and shaking. It seemed like an eternity before the family returned. Africa had left me shell-shocked. When I met Tom five years later I was still carrying these bad memories. It was Tom who helped me get past the trauma.

# 8

# Mr. Laff's and Young Republicans

*Love is life. And if you miss love, you miss life.*

—Leo Buscaglia

I met Tom in 1966. A friend mentioned that there was a social gathering for the Young Republicans at a sports bar called Mr. Laff's. For me to go to a sports bar was perhaps the biggest laugh of all since I had no interest in football, baseball or anything else. My friend explained that it was an enjoyable social event that young Republicans held monthly—and a good way of meeting people.

It was a great evening, lots of socializing and dancing. At the end of the evening, a man offered to drive me home, but my eye was on the tall handsome man standing at the bar. I was determined to introduce myself before leaving and I did. We spoke for a while and I told Tom that I had just returned from visiting my family in Kenya. I invited him to a gathering at my apartment with a group of friends for cocktails and a slide show of my recent safari. Should he be interested, I said, I'd love it if he could join us.

Tom had just graduated from Stanford University Business School and was working for Colgate-Palmolive Company in New York. I was able to get his name and telephone number and went home happy. At 8:45 the next morning, I was at my desk at 550 Fifth Avenue. I answered the phone and to my surprise, it was Tom. He asked me out for dinner that evening and we became inseparable. We met in February and were married January 1, 1967, the following year. His version is that I picked him up in a bar. I guess that is true.

By the time I met Tom, I had been in New York for four years and was already thinking of my next move—to Colorado or San Francisco. As it happened, I had an opportunity for a job in San Francisco, but there was one drawback: I had just met Tom. He suggested that instead of making the move, I visit first. He was going home to the Bay Area for the holidays and asked me to meet his family and spend Christmas with them. I agreed, readily.

### Ready for the Altar

In early December, before visiting Tom's family, I went on a shopping spree. We were so in love, I thought it would be a good idea to be prepared for a wedding. I went to Bergdorf Goodman and bought a smart mini-length brocade dress with a matching coat, very much in fashion. I had just enough money to buy a taffeta bow with a net for my head. It was a Jackie Kennedy look-alike outfit. I had no money left for anything else, so my roommate let me borrow her white silk shoes. I asked the store if I could return the outfit for a full credit if I didn't get married. I felt so organized and happy. I was ready for the altar—unbeknownst to Tom.

Tom called his parents and told them he was dating a girl from Africa and that he would like to bring me home for Christmas. There was silence at the other end of the phone. Tom's parents were very conservative; an African girl was not exactly what the Tusher family had in mind for their son. Obviously, they were in for a big surprise when they finally met me, blue-eyed and fair.

As Christmas was nearing, we did decide to get married. Much to Tom's amazement, I had my dress and was ready for the altar.

The Vietnam War was surging in the mid-1960s. Tom had finished his basic training at Fort Dix and was headed for the Defense Language School in Monterey, California, to learn Russian. I knew we couldn't marry unless I had a job, as being on an army salary was limiting. We went to Carmel, near Monterey, where I interviewed with Ashley Travel Agency and got a job, the only time in our relationship when I was the breadwinner.

We visited many churches in the Bay Area, but no one was able to marry us on such short notice during the Christmas season. Every minister we spoke with undoubtedly thought I was pregnant, which made me break out in a nervous rash. We were fortunate to find St. Clement's Episcopal Church in Berkeley, where a charming minister from Sydney married us at five o'clock on New Year's Day. My family did not know until after the fact, because everything was so last minute. We invited friends and family who were in the area. Tom's brother, Terry, was best man and his wife, Diana, was my bridesmaid.

I had a pass on British Overseas Airways and used it to get back to New York just six hours after we married. Tom and I were apart for the next two weeks. I returned to New York to resign and say my goodbyes, especially to my roommate Phyllis. I returned to San Francisco and we moved to Monterey, where Tom studied Russian in order to interpret secret documents.

During our months in Carmel, we lived in a little cottage. Tom had earphones on for what seemed like all of the time. His Russian language program was hard on both of us but more so for Tom as Russian is a hard language to learn.

Tom had already completed his basic training in October, before we were married. He was called into the Reserves at Fort Dix, New Jersey, for eight intensive weeks, but he was never called up. In one of his letters, he told me that some young men died of meningitis during the training, which was conducted in brutal weather conditions.

## Meeting the Parents

A year after we were married, we decided to visit my mother and Eric in Malawi, a small landlocked country south of Tanzania. I had told Tom stories about my mother, but he had never met anyone in my family. We arrived after thirty hours of travel. Eric met us at the airport without Mummy. When we arrived home, she appeared, covered in bruises. She called me aside and proceeded to tell me how Eric had beaten her the night before. I was both devastated and speechless; nothing had changed. I had been so excited to introduce my husband to my mother and her partner, and that is how they welcomed us. Having heard my stories about my mother's abandonment, Tom held a negative opinion of her from the start. This trip cemented his view.

After Malawi, we flew to Tanzania and met friends who gave us their yellow Volkswagen bug to use. Imagine us, two tall people, folding in and out of a tiny car as we drove through the African savanna. We then went to Dar es Salaam, the largest city in Tanzania and its capital, to visit Daddy. This was Tom's first visit with my father. Before getting married, Tom never had the opportunity to ask him for my hand in marriage, so it was good to finally bring the two important men in my life together. But Dar es Salaam was so rundown and poor. The only fun thing we did was to visit a friend of Daddy's who lived on the beach and had two cheetahs as pets. It was sad, though, as they were caged and when let out were on long chains.

I was anxious to say our goodbyes and return home.

# 9
# Living in San Juan

*Don't let life discourage you. Everyone who got where*
*he is had to begin where he was.*

—Robert L. Evans

After Tom finished at the language school, we moved back
to New York with Colgate-Palmolive, where we lived
briefly on the West Side in the Eighties. Next came our
transfer to San Juan, Puerto Rico, where Tom was a
product manager for Colgate. Life in San Juan was fun,
but, at times, dangerous.

We rented the top floor of our landlord's house, one
block from the beach. Luckily, the landlord had a standard
poodle named Baby and she would accompany me to the
beach and never take her eyes off me. She was wonderful,
and it was a good thing I had her because some of the
Puerto Rican men were not to be trusted. I remember one

frightening time when I was watched by a group of men who tried to close in on me while I was sunbathing on the beach. More than once, when I went into the ocean, they stole my towel and possessions. But they did not do this with Baby, the poodle, sitting as my guard.

During this time we drove a British racing green convertible Triumph. The steering wheel and boot and bonnet had to be chained down and locked at night, or the car would be stripped by morning. We awoke one morning to find the car on blocks and the tires missing.

I worked in the industrial part of San Juan at an advertising agency. It took an hour to get there on a standing-room-only bus that was tightly packed. I held on tightly to the straps up above, swaying in the humidity and heat. Meanwhile, Tom was working in Old San Juan and driving to work each morning in our cute green Triumph with the top down, feeling very happy. When we could, we drove around Puerto Rico and traveled to a few of the other Caribbean islands. How amazing it was that our first overseas transfer was to the Caribbean. One of my greatest wishes had already come true so early in my marriage.

We didn't like Puerto Rico, but to fit in with the Spanish-speaking people, Tom took Spanish lessons at Berlitz. However, the Puerto Ricans seemed insulted when he spoke Spanish and they replied only in English. It happened that one of the instructors had a client who was being transferred to Nairobi and he heard from Tom that I spoke Swahili, so I was asked to give this man a crash course. A crash course it was! The man spoke many languages and there was a point where I was unable to keep up with him because he was such a quick study. I was relieved when I heard he was being transferred early.

Meanwhile, Tom was anxious for a career change, so he made several appointments to interview with other companies—Gillette in Boston, Johnson & Johnson in New Jersey, and McKinsey Consulting in New York City, among others. A friend suggested he contact Levi Strauss. This appealed to us because it was headquartered in San Francisco.

Tom had been offered several jobs, but San Francisco seemed to be pulling the hardest at his heartstrings. When he was offered the job, I was slightly apprehensive because I had never heard of Levi Strauss. Having lived in New York and worked near the garment district, my impression of the industry wasn't all that favorable. But Tom saw it as another consumer-brand marketing opportunity.

I found San Francisco to be beautiful and sophisticated. Soon after joining Levi's, Tom was transferred to Mexico to fill in for the general manager who had had a heart attack. It was only a six-month assignment, so I stayed in San Francisco because I had been offered a job with Pakistan International Airlines. I worked for a wonderful man in an office on the corner of Geary and Powell

Streets that overlooked Union Square.

I had interviewed with many airlines when we arrived in San Francisco, starting with American Airlines and then moving down the alphabet—BOAC, Cathay Pacific, Delta, Eastern, Frontier—all to no avail. When I got to the letter "P," I was finally successful.

# 10

# San Francisco

*Be sure to wear some flowers in your hair.*

—Scott McKenzie

I had no idea that there were so many Pakistanis living in California. At that time, many of them, immigrants to our country, lived near Sacramento and grew rice. Working with them on their flight arrangements posed challenges. They wanted large discounts and could not understand that I personally was unable to make that happen. And when it came time to pay, like the Jamaican customers in New York, they would empty their pockets of all their coins and one-dollar bills. If I was lucky, they had fives and tens. It was time consuming and I had to recount the money several times as they often tried to cut me short. The good news was the job allowed me fifty-percent off airfare and hotel rooms, so Tom and I could travel comfortably on weekends to Bali and other exotic places.

In 1969, when Tom and I moved to San Francisco with Levi Strauss, we found an apartment at 2220 Pacific Avenue, between Webster and Buchanan. We spent considerable time going to consignment stores and looking at advertisements for old and used furniture. One of our prized pieces was our dining table—a wagon wheel. We used the hub as our nightly candleholder. Who knows how far across the country it had traveled? I wondered what it would say if only it could speak.

While living here, we brought Malcie and Gregory to San Francisco with the idea of helping them get into college. Tom thought he might be able to get them into the University of California at Berkeley. They had never traveled beyond East Africa, so San Francisco was a big step for them.

I will never forget meeting them at the airport. They were in khaki shorts, long khaki socks and white shirts. They looked, quite frankly, like white hunters. Malcie got off the plane with a *samburu* sword six feet long—a gift for us from Tanzania. Can you imagine walking onto a plane with a sword today? Malcie and Gregory spoke many African dialects and I appreciated the bartering that probably took place when they bought the sword. Both were in desperate need of a shower. They smelled so bad, I felt for the other passengers. I don't think my brothers knew anything about deodorant.

San Francisco was the epicenter of the hippie movement and Union Square was a gathering spot. I would pass them in the street, the men with long hair and beards, the women in long, loose-fitting dresses with flowers in their hair. They were free spirits, anti-establishment, against nuclear weapons and the Vietnam War, in favor of drugs and free sex. Many took psychedelic drugs to expand their consciousness and lived in communes as part of their lifestyle. Their watchwords were peace, love and personal freedom. When Gregory and Malcolm arrived, this movement was in full force and, in the People's Republic of Berkeley, centered on the Cal campus.

Malcolm and Gregory stayed with us for a month. During the days they would come to my office. In the afternoon they would sightsee, taking the cable car to Fisherman's Wharf, walking through the alleys of Chinatown, or enjoying the pasta in North Beach.

Their favorite haunt was Macy's. They had never seen revolving or automatic doors. Stepping onto escalators was a challenge, but they mastered it and spent hours each day going up and down. It was so much fun to see them do things they had never done before.

At the end of their visit, they thanked us for the opportunity to come to the United States and go to school—but they didn't like the hippie movement. The US was not what they had expected. There was too much "free spirit" for my brothers. We had hoped they would attend college here, but it was not what they wanted. They told us they felt more comfortable in East Africa than San Francisco. They loved the kind of freedom they felt in Africa.

## 11

# The Move to Down Under

*A new beginning. And things will change.*

—Taylor Swift

Later that year, Tom was transferred to Sydney to open the first Levi Strauss office in Australia. It was very flattering that they appointed Tom for this job, as he was only twenty-nine years old. It took us some time to find a house we could afford, but eventually we bought our first home at 141 Cremorne Road, on the North Shore in Cremorne. Tom's office was out near the airport, about a forty-five-minute commute from home. The neighbors were not welcoming, and I remember feeling lonely and isolated. I rarely saw Tom, who often didn't come home until ten o'clock in the evening. I would keep his dinner warm and he would frequently fall asleep from exhaustion while trying to eat.

Australia proved difficult for me. I didn't like it from the beginning. For one thing, Australian men were party boys and they put themselves before their families. This did not work well for us. At the same time, the culture was Victorian. At parties the men would be in one corner and the women in another, as if the women were invisible. After dinner, the men would retire to the drawing room to drink many ports and smoke cigars. Tom knew I did not enjoy this kind of an evening out and therefore we didn't do it very often. This lifestyle was not what we were used to in San Francisco.

But there were good things happening as well. Tom was very happy in his job starting up production in Adelaide. Levi's Australian business became the most profitable international company.

I had been offered a job with American Airlines, which was a thrill for me. But I was even more thrilled to find out I was pregnant with Gregory, our first child, so I declined the job offer and happily prepared to be a mother.

## Motherhood

On September 15, 1971, the contractions started. It was 4:30 P.M. and rush hour. King George Hospital was out near the airport, not too far from Tom's office. I called Tom and he suggested I take a taxi; he would meet me at the hospital. I will never forget carrying my overnight bag and wearing a very smart navy maternity dress trimmed in white. I looked like I was off to work rather than a hospital. But I felt attractive. The taxi driver was a woman who spent forty minutes telling me horror stories about her first delivery. She said she hoped I had a better delivery than she had had.

The scene before me at the hospital was unsettling. All the wards were full, and women in labor, mostly Italians and Greeks, lined the hospital corridor two abreast on both sides of the aisle. They were all moaning and crying. I wondered what I was in for!

I had private insurance, which meant I got a private room. However, the head nurse was a real witch. She told Tom to leave, because he couldn't possibly be helpful. She promised him that the doctor would call as soon as our baby was on the way. I had gone through the Lamaze training method to have a natural childbirth. But as the contractions increased, I was not allowed even a sip of water and was given instead a damp cloth to put in my mouth. That made me gag. I was in back-aching labor for twelve hours. Nurse Ratchet would come in to tell me that I was never going to make it through natural childbirth. "If you think puffing and panting is going to help you relieve pain, you are wrong," she said in her unkind bedside manner.

I had been adamant about not having an epidural. But the pain was intense and when I saw the needle, I gave in.

It was a painless delivery and we had a beautiful baby boy who weighed in at six pounds, eleven ounces. Tom walked into my room at seven-thirty in the morning and I asked him if he knew we had a son. He did not. No one had bothered to call him, which we still can't believe to this day. We were both so hurt and tried hard not to let it spoil the experience of being with our firstborn. We had difficulty naming our son, but I loved the names Gregory and Malcolm, because I loved my twin brothers so much. We agreed to name our baby Gregory Malcolm Tusher.

## Chubby Little Legs

When I was pregnant with Gregory, I wanted so badly to be a loving and caring mother. I talked to my unborn baby and told him so. Still, there were many times when all I did was cry. I was afraid that I would turn out like my own mother. But that was never the case. I loved motherhood from the start and it brought me nothing but joy. The love I felt was intense and deep.

On business or home-leave trips back to San Francisco, we would stop at different Pacific islands—American Samoa, Western Samoa, Tonga, Fiji, New Caledonia, Bora Bora, Moorea, Rarotonga and the Hawaiian Islands.

Gregory was such a happy, loveable, easy baby. The island natives loved him and would scoop him up and squeeze his chubby little legs. Many times, he would pull his leg away when he saw a native coming towards him for fear of being squeezed, but we were never at a loss for babysitters.

When Gregory was eighteen months old, we went to New Zealand on a business trip. Tom had opened Levi's New Zealand with an office in Auckland and a production facility in Christchurch. We were staying in the Heron Hotel and Tom said, "I need a haircut. I'll be back in an hour or less."

At a nearby putting green, Gregory and I went out to hit some balls, expecting Tom back momentarily. Two, three, four, five hours later Tom had not returned. By this time I was trying hard to contain my emotion, as I didn't want our son to sense my fear.

At 8:30, Tom returned sheepishly, but with a smile on his face, apologizing for being so late.

The barber and Tom had been sharing stories about fishing, and he asked Tom if he would like to go catch a few. Before Tom knew it, the shop curtain was rolled down, a closed sign put up, and away they went. They had a great afternoon.

Much to our delight, I was expecting again. When I was pregnant with Gregory, I had asked the doctor if it was possible that I might be carrying twins. Having twins was at the top of my wish list. But the answer was "no" with Gregory. This time the doctor looked at me and said, "Pauline, you will need twin prams." I was overjoyed. With Tom traveling, I finally introduced myself to some neighbors in case I needed someone in an emergency. One neighbor told me they had been watching us from their kitchen window, but were too embarrassed to knock on our door and introduce themselves. This was so Aussie!

We had a German shepherd pup named Tara, and she, Gregory and I would go to Balmoral Beach on a regular basis. One day when we were at the beach, I started to hemorrhage, but I didn't want to scare Gregory. We hurried home and I called my ob-gyn immediately. His wife answered the phone. Calm, yet cold, she advised me to go to bed.

Tom was on a business trip and I was alone. We had to get a nanny to take care of Gregory, as the doctor advised me to stay in bed for the next three months. I was lucky to find a wonderful young English lady—someone so good to us and to our son.

Tom was in San Francisco when I was rushed to the hospital by ambulance. There I gave birth to twins, a stillborn daughter and son. I had so hoped for a girl and a boy.

In those days, they just took the stillborn babies from you and no one talked about it. There was never mention of a burial, naming our little ones, or anything that would help with closure and grieving. I was on my own and didn't know what to do. It took me more than two years to stop crying. I was a closet crier; I didn't want Tom to see me like that. He is a compassionate man, but even

Tom didn't understand the depth of my emotions. It was a very painful time for me.

Still, while living in Sydney we did have some terrific trips with Gregory, who was a wonderful traveler. Most were for business, some for pleasure. We luxuriated in the soft sand and warm blue waters among friendly islanders, who especially loved children.

Tom thought it would be great fun to have a Chinese junk in Sydney so we could sail up through the Great Barrier Reef. With his contacts in Hong Kong he had one built for us, changing the dimensions to accommodate tall people. We were very excited when she arrived in Neutral Bay. Tom, his friend Bob Hill, and the captain Walt spent many hours putting ballast into the boat and fine-tuning her. Captain Walt took care of everything else, including the plans for many of our sailing trips.

Once, we sailed up to the Great Barrier Reef with Bob and Robin Hill with their two young daughters and Gregory. We all had the best time. Neil Diamond was the choice of music, and we would crank him up as we enjoyed our cocktails or fishing or just being lazy. Tom foolishly had string around his big toe, using it as fishing line in shark-infested water. Fortunately, no shark ever struck. What was he thinking?

We were the talk of Sydney. Ours was the only junk in the harbor—the only one in Australia for that matter. When we sailed up the Great Barrier Reef, people thought they were dreaming when they saw us. Perhaps they thought it was a Chinese invasion!

One day we pulled into Dunk Island, which we thought was deserted until we saw an elderly lady walking slowly to the beach with her multi-colored floral parasol.

She had obviously dressed in a hurry. She sported a well-worn floral green dress and bright red lipstick that was smeared around her lips. Her husband, Bill, came out on a barge to pick us up and when we arrived at the beach, he lowered a ramp to keep our feet from getting wet and took us ashore. He was a wiry fellow, well tanned with gray unkempt hair and a thin gray moustache.

Thrilled to have visitors, the woman introduced herself as Noreen and couldn't stop talking. Although she had initially feared she was being invaded, she was very relieved to meet us.

They invited us into their thatched hut, which was

full of shell necklaces, shells and sharks' teeth. On the wall was a photo of an aircraft carrier. From what we understood, Bill had been in the war off the Queensland coast in the Coral Sea. Shot down, he had managed to get on some debris and paddled for days until he reached a reef and was rescued.

After the war, Bill vowed he would return and live on Dunk Island with his wife. They built their thatched hut and lived like hermits for years. They loved our company and were very sorry to see us return to the junk and sail away.

We went to islands that were, at the time, completely deserted (like Lizard) and finally sailed to Heyman Island, which had a small hotel. Our feet finally on terra firma, we were all ready for a long shower, a good meal, and a comfortable bed to sleep in. As we arrived, there was a cyclone warning, so we were confined to the lounge area. We had to put sheets along the windows and lie low for many hours. The wind was ferocious and the windows cracked from flying debris, but thankfully, they didn't shatter and no one was hurt. The next day we returned to the junk, which was covered in salt and took hours to spray down.

### Blanket Bay

After Tom opened the New Zealand office in 1971, he visited the office in Auckland, then went to Queenstown for a marketing trip. Tom has always enjoyed looking at real estate, so he spoke to an agent who suggested that he look at two properties, time permitting, both on the north end of Queenstown's Lake Wakatipu. There was no road apart from a farm track, which traversed many rivers and gullies, so the agent drove Tom there in her four-wheel drive. Rental cars were not permitted. It took two-and-a-half hours to get to Blanket Bay, a property that had been on the market for many years. It was a warm, sunny day with a bright blue sky and majestic mountains all around—a realtor's dream. The lake was smooth as glass. Tom fell immediately for the fifity-two freehold acres on the shore of the lake.

Tom came back to Sydney and said he had bought the property. I couldn't believe it. New Zealand was a beautiful country, as it is today, but it was also a boring, sleepy place. You could not get a good meal or bottle of wine, everything shut down at 5:00 sharp, and there was no shopping on Saturday or Sunday. I asked Tom what we were going to do with the property. His idea was to build a hut on the edge of the lake where, when retired, we could spend several weeks each year, fishing, hiking and reading. I was not happy, and knew we would return to San Francisco and never go back to New Zealand. Most importantly, we were just thirty-one years old and could not afford it. Tom proposed we pay it off over five years and the sellers agreed. Doing the math he realized he would have increments in his salary to make this possible. What a visionary! It was the only freehold property along a forty-mile stretch of lakefront; the rest of the land is all crown or leasehold.

Over the years, we allowed our neighboring farmers to graze sheep on Blanket Bay. Then, about three years before retiring, we decided to build a home on the property. We were no longer hut people. Finally, we made up our minds to build a year-round lodge rather than a home. Today, Blanket Bay is a travel destination—an award-winning, five-star lodge on the edge of Lake Wakitupu, a stunning setting with mountains to the east and west. Many of our guests fly to Milford Sound and take a twelve-minute helicopter ride to get there.

I had always said I wanted to marry a farmer. That didn't happen, but we did buy Wyuna Station, a 40,000-acre ranch adjacent to Blanket Bay, where we have cattle, sheep and deer for venison. I guess I did end up with a farmer after all!

I had always loved horses so Tom bought me my first, Isabella (Bella), a palomino, followed by Bayley, Sierra and many more over the years. This was yet another dream that has come true for me.

## 12

# Goodbye Sydney, Hello London

*The best thing to hold on to in life is each other.*
—Audrey Hepburn

We had been in Sydney for four years when Tom received a call from the head office, saying they wanted him in the London office where there were financial problems. Although I had been unhappy at the beginning of our tenure in Sydney, by now we were both enjoying Australia and the Sydney lifestyle. We had just bought a new home on the waterfront overlooking the Opera House; we loved our Chinese junk and we finally felt settled. The thought of moving to England and getting a company out of the red, which would mean more long hours for Tom, was not appealing to us. We thought seriously about going into the restaurant business in Sydney, but the head office put pressure on Tom. They told him to find his "flexible hat," which he did. So, once again, it was time to move on.

Still, I could now cross another wish off of my list; I had lived in the Caribbean and in the Pacific and seen some of its glorious islands. How amazing is life that I should be granted another wish so few years later?

The move went well, except for one problem: Tom had bought a case of Penfolds red wine in 1971, the year Gregory was born, and we were going to open a bottle in 1992 on Greg's twenty-first birthday. When we got to London, everything was there except the wine. Looking back, had Tom not mentioned to the movers who were packing our household items to make sure the wine was well packed because it was so good, it might have arrived in London.

We rented a small apartment on Hill Street, a few blocks from Grosvenor Square. Tom was commuting to Northampton, which was two hours each way. Between his long hours and the black ice in winter, we decided it would be better to move there. So we rented a home in Northampton. But once again, I was lonely. I hated it really—nothing to do.

We returned to London to a lovely home in Kensington at 8 St. Albans Grove, renting the four-story townhouse from the Guinness family of Guinness stout fame, who had been transferred to South Africa. In the basement there was a kitchen, family room and laundry room opening onto a small garden. On the main level was a formal dining room with a dumbwaiter to the kitchen and a formal living room. Two floors up were the bedrooms and, to be sure, there was a lot of running up and down the stairs. We had an intercom system to hear the children—Gregory was four and Scott was due in November. The Guinnesses had left their furniture, a collection of very fine antiques. Tom had relocated the northern European office to London and it turned out the new office was only two minutes away. It was a wonderful contrast to his previous commutes.

I am not sure how it came to be, but Dad moved to London after living forty years in East Africa, and when we lived in London in 1974 we saw each other again. I do not remember how we tracked each other down. We lived in Kensington and Dad was in Nottinghill Gate. We were never invited to his home; his private life was a mystery. He didn't talk much and never complained. I had never received a letter from him saying how difficult times were. We had him over for dinner every week and would slip him fifteen pounds as it appeared he was struggling. How the tables had turned. Uncle Eric had helped me in London and now I was able to do the same for Daddy.

Daddy worked in Holborn for a jeweler who bought and sold gold. Tom took me there and bought for me two lovely gold necklaces, which Dad was able to sell to us at a good price. I remember leaving in a taxi and looking through the back window, waving goodbye to Daddy. I knew then I would not see him again.

In 1977, while living in Ross, we received a telegram saying Daddy had died of throat cancer, the same thing my sister Pat would die of in 2004. Dad was a heavy pipe smoker and drinker—and the combination is deadly. When I think of my father I see his sweet smile, the twinkle in his eye, and his pipe always in his mouth.

Scott would be born in London, and I didn't want any surprises. I decided in advance that I wanted to be induced and told Tom that this time I wanted him close by. The night before we checked into my room at the hospital, we went to La Grenouille, a very elegant restaurant in London. My doctor said I could have wine and he told me to enjoy it. Michael Scott was born the next morning, November 5, 1975, at 6:50 A.M. It was Guy Fawkes Day and coincidentally, my doctor's name was Guy and his son was Guy too. He told us we should call our son Guy, and I laughed and told him that it was out of the question because it wouldn't work in America. We now had two sons, one Australian and one English. Gregory was very sweet to his new brother.

Contrasting the joy we felt with our growing family was the stress of knowing the Irish Republican Army was bombing so close to where we lived. The IRA had adopted a strategy of violence to achieve its goal of a united Ireland. We were afraid to walk past mailboxes that might explode; restaurants were shielded with heavy mesh wiring to deflect hand grenades. When we traveled by air, we had to identify our suitcases on the tarmac before boarding. Many years before the threat of suicide bombers, authorities assumed no one would bomb a plane they were flying on.

We were thrilled when Tom was transferred back to the head office in San Francisco. He had been very successful, and made the UK and Scandinavian businesses profitable.

I stayed in London as Tom made several visits to the Bay Area to look for housing. He looked in Hillsborough, Orinda and Marin, but had not found anything he liked. It was my turn to look, so I left the boys with our nanny and looked at eight to twelve houses a day for a week. Tom saw an ad that read, "Sylvan setting, pond and pool in Ross." We had never heard of Ross, but he wanted me to see the house.

I loved the setting, but not the house. When Tom saw it, he realized the potential if we made some additions. Tom has such a good eye; it was the perfect house for us. We moved back to California into our new home in June 1976. Scott was seven months and Gregory was nearly five. We have added on to the house over the years and have tweaked the garden, adding a 125-foot waterfall in the back.

# 13

# Gregory and Scott Visit
# My East African Roots

*Don't forget who you are and where you come from.*

—F. Scott Fitzgerald

Every year Tom and I took Gregory and Scott on an overseas holiday. As Gregory was born in Sydney and Scott in London, we visited their roots. In 1984, we wanted them to see mine, so we flew from San Francisco to Nairobi via Lagos. It took thirty-two hours—a long trip for Scott who was eight and Gregory who was twelve.

There had been so many changes in Nairobi, it wasn't easy to find my old stomping grounds. We had a driver, who was Kikuyu, and it wasn't too long into the trip that I began to have an uncomfortable feeling that his father could have been in the Mau Mau. I wanted to show the children where I was nearly killed with a panga in Daddy's vegetable garden. I wanted them to see the home where the horses were burned alive and the police station where I slept the night the Rucks were murdered. The driver knew I spoke Swahili and I didn't like the look in his eyes. In the end, I decided to skip showing the children the horror show that had been my life as a teenager.

We went to see a hippo pool, where we stopped for a picnic in Tsavo National Park. In no time we were surrounded by cheeky monkeys. They were so inquisitive and tried hard to get into our picnic baskets. Naughtily, I gave them a tube of toothpaste and they became quite amused by it. One monkey ran up a tree to figure out what was in the tube. The next thing we knew, toothpaste oozed out all over his body. We laughed as he tried to shake the paste off his body and hands.

We stayed at Samburu Game Lodge, where we saw some amazing birds, all sizes and colors, and other wildlife. One evening we were finishing dinner and Gregory and Scott asked if they could return to our cabin. We agreed, but it was dark, and we told them they had to stay on the path and not stray. Three minutes later, a panicked *askari* (guide) told the guests that he had seen a pride of lions on the property a few feet from the lodge, heading toward the cabins. They warned us not to leave the main lodge unescorted. Our hearts nearly stopped; our immediate reaction was panic and we had the askari take us immediately to our cabin to make sure the boys were okay.

As luck had it, the lions had found a herd of buffalo, right behind our cabin. Gregory and Scott were watching them through the window as the lions closed in on a wounded buffalo for the kill. Four buffalo tried to protect their buddy, but the lions were more aggressive. It was fascinating, but difficult to watch. After some time and a skirmish, six lions brought the buffalo down. We still tremble when we think of the boys walking just a few feet from the lions, which were fortunately distracted by the buffalo.

We went on to the Mt. Kenya Safari Club in the Aberdare on the slopes of majestic Mt. Kenya.

It was originally a retreat for Hollywood stars (William Holden was a part owner) and our boys loved everything about it. They were free to run around without the fear of lions. The lodge was set on 100 acres of beautifully landscaped gardens. There was an indoor swimming pool, which the boys indulged in.

The Maasai women and men who entertained us with chants and ancient rhythmic dances delighted us. The Maasai are tall and slim with very long legs and can jump several feet into the air. They wear a red cloth wrapped around the body over one shoulder and adorn themselves with bright beaded necklaces. Their hair is covered in cow fat and mud and then braided and pulled back. Their lovely smiles show their white teeth.

Children had to eat at 6:00 P.M. and not with their

parents—a throwback from colonial days when children were to be seen and not heard. The children had to dress up in khaki pants, blue blazers and dress shoes. Flip-flops were a definite "no-no." Dinner was in the formal dining room, where waiters wearing white kanzus attended them. After serving the boys, they stood at attention around the room, ready to jump when the young guests wanted something. Gregory and Scott thought this was such fun to have so many servants waiting on them.

We also stayed at Treetops in the Aberdare Mountains, a lovely, rustic lodge built into a tree with a deck surrounding it. The lodge overlooked a watering hole with salt licks that attracted all kinds of animals. We would be having tea or a cocktail and watch in amazement as game wandered in to get a drink. But we had to watch out for the thieving monkeys that would come into rooms and steal things. We were warned ahead of time to hide our wallets, passports and anything else of value.

# 14
# Roots Revisited

*Though the road's been rocky, it sure feels good to me.*

—Bob Marley

For many years, I felt I had to return to Tanzania to visit Nic and Sylvie Emmanuel, my Greek friends from Moshi. But every time Tom and I thought about it, something else came up. We finally decided I couldn't put it off any longer, and I traveled to Tanzania in September of 2011. Because Tom couldn't come, he wanted my brother Malcolm to join me, so I wouldn't be in Tanzania on my own. Malcie asked if he could bring his sixteen-year-old son, my nephew, Mathew, whom I had not yet met. I thought this was a great idea. I flew over from San Francisco and they flew up from Durban, South Africa, where they lived.

I arrived three days before my family. Nic and Sylvie met me at the Kilimanjaro Airport. We had not seen each other in forty years, but other than all of us aging, they were still the same. The same smiles, the same mannerisms, the same voice and the same spirit; it was like going back in time to visit very dear friends. It seemed like I had seen them yesterday. Chattering nonstop, we arrived at their home, the same one I used to visit in the foothills of Kilimanjaro when I was a teenager. We were having afternoon tea and catching up when I mentioned to Nic that I had come for a reason, but I was too emotional to explain it. It would have to wait until the next day.

Nic, meanwhile, was pointing to the sky. "Look, Paulie," he said in his familiar Greek accent. He told me to look even higher, and then I saw it: Kilimanjaro. The clouds had cleared and I saw the top of the mountain that inspired so much dreaming in my youth. It was such a moving moment to view Kili again in that way, it brought tears to my eyes. I was overwhelmed with emotion. So much had happened since I had last seen the top of this beautiful mountain. Quickly the clouds came in and covered her up again. It was as if the mountain wanted to let me know it was still there. It had opened up briefly to welcome me, and that was it. I didn't see its snow-covered top again until Mathew and Malcie arrived.

The next day we went on a tour in Moshi. We went back to our old homes, the boys' school, the telephone exchange, the insurance office and the swimming pool. The municipality was no longer maintaining the town and nothing was in order; everything was grimy, dusty, and in total chaos, unlike the colonial days when everything was whitewashed.

Today, in Moshi, a lot of people have motorbikes, but there are no rules and no helmets, so there are many fatal accidents. It was nerve-racking to drive on the road. The train station today is derelict and covered with graffiti. Trains no longer run. Moshi did not match the memories of my youth in colonial Africa when buildings were maintained. Jacaranda trees no longer line the avenues.

When Nic and Sylvie drove me to West Kilimanjaro, where Tania Carr and my friend Annabel had lived, I was able for a brief time to recall the old days when the British landowners had wonderful, sweeping estates with miles of flat plains and rolling hills, and where I used to ride horseback as a girl.

We were in lion country, so we had to be very careful, as we were back then. Sylvie brought a picnic, and like in the old days, we stopped in the middle of nowhere, dropped down the back of the car and had a lunch of homemade bread, sliced tomatoes and cheese. The odd Maasai tribesman would walk by. For a couple of hours I was in the Africa of my adolescence.

We returned to Lambo Estate where Nic and Sylvie still live. It was sundowner time and we sat, once again, on the terrace. We all had a drink. I then took a deep breath and told Nic, "I am here in Africa to say thank you for helping me leave Tanzania." Nic was clearly puzzled. The Vespa purchase was something that I had thought about for many years, but Nic didn't even remember. I told him I had wanted to come back and thank him for buying my Vespa, which enabled me to leave Tanzania for London. I had to say it looking into his eyes; a letter would never do.

Before leaving San Francisco, I looked everywhere for an appropriate card to give to Nic and lo and behold, I found *the* one—it had a red Vespa on the cover. My Vespa was grey, but that didn't matter. I wrote my license plate (MS 4412) and a note inside:

*Dear Nic,*

*Thank you for helping me leave Tanzania during a hard time in 1959. You were so generous by giving me fifty pounds for my scooter, which was much more than it was worth. You told me you wanted it to ride around the shamba. Thanks to you, Nic, I was able to move forward and start a new chapter in my life. I love you so much for that. I had to fly from San Francisco to Moshi to look in your eyes and hug you, and tell you that I have always appreciated what you did for me and I love you. Thank you again, dear Nic. You gave me my wings.*

Nic poured more wine and by now we were all very emotional. Not a dry eye among us. We took many photos with Nic holding the scooter card I had given him. It was Sylvie's birthday and she cooked a delicious dinner—a fish Nic had caught, homegrown vegetables, and a Pavlova cake for dessert with berries from the garden.

Malcolm and Mathew were with us, but we were running out of time. How grateful I feel to have these friendships that have spanned a lifetime and a globe. When I saw one of the photos we had taken, I was amazed to see we were stand-ing in front of a painting of Kilimanjaro. A fitting memory.

## Safari with Malcie and Mathew

After saying goodbye to the Emmanuels, Malcie, Mathew and I went on safari for eight days. Our first stop was rustic Mdonya Camp, just what I wanted to remind me of the past and to show Malcie and Mathew what I had experienced with my friends. The camp was on the edge of a dry riverbed. During the day the elephants passed our tents and could charge if aggravated, so we were not allowed to go to the dining tent without a Maasai askari. Then after a meal we had to be escorted back again.

One night, at 3:00 A.M., I needed to go to the loo but heard a crashing sound outside my tent. When I looked out, I saw two elephants right there—one pulling at a large branch and the other on the opposite side of the tent, maybe two yards from me. I was in desperate need to visit the bathroom, but lay frozen in my bed, not wanting to disturb them. I willed them to go away.

The window was open but covered with netting to keep bugs out. I could see clearly. The elephant turned its head and stared in the window for what seemed like an eternity.

He stared at me and I stared back, wishing he would move on. A few minutes later, he and his friend did. Meanwhile, I could hear the lions roaring and the impalas mating in the distance. These are the sounds in the night that visit you on safari.

At daybreak we had great game runs before breakfast and again before dinner. It gets dark consistently at seven-thirty in the evening, and at seven o'clock we would have cocktails and meet with other guests. There was no electricity in the camp or the tents—just kerosene lanterns, which weren't strong enough to read by. We would return to our tents by nine o'clock, which made for a long night without light.

The staff was not well trained and the management was not managing very well, so it was hard for them to know what to do. At breakfast we couldn't get to the honey or jams because they didn't cover the jars and bees would swarm *en masse.*

Nevertheless, there was something wonderful about the mornings. Each morning we were greeted with tea delivered to our tents. "Jambo memsahib, your chai is here." Then we were escorted to the dining tent for breakfast.

After breakfast we boarded jeeps for the game run. We did see a lot of game. We would stop on riverbanks for morning tea and watch lions resting near water and the pheasants, quails and other game passing by. There is no other experience like it in the world.

We then flew to Selous Safari Camp, one of the least

known, yet largest conservation areas in Tanzania. The landscape was different, but still magnificent, scattered with baobabs, one of nature's oldest and oddest trees. Also known as the upside down tree, the baobab is as stark as it is beautiful. It retains water in its trunk, so during a drought, elephants are still able to find water by pulling the bark away. We really enjoyed our guide as well as the staff. Once again at night, the askari had to escort us to our tents. This was a blessing because nights were total darkness. One night after dinner, the askari noticed a hippo five feet in front of us. Hippos are very vicious. The guide shouted, "*Samama*" ("stand still") in Swahili. We froze. We gave the hippo his right of way and finally went back to our tents.

In the morning I awoke to a "*Jambo*," which means hello in Swahili. Tea was at six-thirty and the next thing I heard was a bang: a very handsome giraffe was on my terrace reaching for high branches on a tree. I watched as the precious creature nibbled away. Later that afternoon we went out on a boat cruise to watch the hippos and crocodiles. We turned a corner to find a dead hippo on the bank and a family of lions enjoying a hippo dinner. We saw hundreds of crocodiles competing for hippo meat, and our guides told us the oldest crocodiles were first in the pecking order and the younger ones further out in the lake.

We returned to the lodge and had a delicious dinner beneath the stars. Malcie and I had a lot of catching up with the many years we had missed and shared the moments of the day. It was wonderful getting to know Mathew. Each day had been magical and was what I needed—a taste of Africa again. I had missed it for many years. I was so grateful to Tom for letting me do this with my brother and nephew. It will stay with me forever.

## Mummy

"Don't forget to bring Mummy," I reminded Malcie, before he and Mathew met me in Tanzania.

Mummy had died in her sleep in 2005, at the age of 92 in Port Elizabeth, South Africa, and wanted her ashes scattered on Mt. Kilimanjaro, in the Indian Ocean, and in London to be with her family. We knew she would have been thrilled we were going to put her plan into action.

I had longed to understand my mother better, but it was not to be. In 1995, when Tom had a business trip to Cape Town, I went two weeks ahead of him to spend time with her. I brought a tape recorder, hoping she would record her story. Mummy would have nothing to do with it. All I had hoped for in those two weeks was for my mother to reach out and say, "Paulie, I am sorry for the pain I caused you." I just wanted to cry it out of my system, but it didn't happen. Although Tom never saw Mother again, I saw her in London and we spoke regularly by phone. Tom helped her financially for many years, which was so generous given the circumstances. When she died, she left no letters for her family. I had so hoped for one.

Scattering her ashes would provide a different kind of closure.

Malcie arrived in Moshi with what looked like a grey brick. We had not seen each other for twenty years, and because I had never met my nephew, Mathew, it was an emotional welcoming at Mt. Kilimanjaro airport. With Mummy in her box in the back, Malcie and I revisited our old homes, where he and Gregory used to drag rhino skulls and animals into our garden. Malcolm, being ten years younger than I, had an amazing memory for finding the places that were part of our lives.

We planned a day driving to Mawenzi on Kilimanjaro where we would shed a third of Mummy's ashes. I used to ride there on my scooter with my two five-year-old brothers sitting behind me. This time, while we were driving up, it seemed like such a far distance that I couldn't imagine how I did it as a teenager—on a scooter carrying twins on corrugated roads with enormous potholes and through villages. We arrived at our destination to find a lodge, where we had lunch. We then set out on a hike through the rainforest to see the waterfall where we used to go so many years ago. We stood in the falls and felt it was a befitting spot to say goodbye to Mummy—a third of her, that is. Malcie did all the talking as Mathew and I looked on. We had completed the first of our mother's wishes for her remains.

I had not seen my friend Annabel for thirty years. We set out to visit her at her thatched bungalow, a three-bedroom B&B hideaway on the Indian Ocean in Pangani, an hour north of Tanzania's port city of Tanga. After two hours of fixed-wing planes and an hour-and-a-half by taxi, Malcie, Mathew and I finally arrived.

The Indian Ocean was our destination. On our rented dhow, we sailed to a sandbar where we anchored and ate our picnic lunch. Walking through the warm, crystal-clear water, we scattered more of the ashes and said more goodbyes. Mummy would have loved this—to be in a dhow and then scattered in the winds.

Annabelle wanted us to see her friends' home, which was under construction. There was a deadly snake in one of the rooms, which unsettled me and brought back bad memories. Also, people were drinking so much as they socialized that I strangely felt out of place. I had a sharp realization that while I loved being back in Africa, I knew I no longer belonged. I felt ready to leave and get back home to Tom.

Malcie, Mathew and I were preparing to say our good-byes. We flew together to Zanzibar for a five-hour layover. We were moving at a fast clip through narrow, dirty streets filled with hawkers—with no time to visit the resorts.

We flew to Lamu, a beautiful island that was once an important trade center like Zanzibar in East Africa. As we strolled through narrow streets, dating back to the 12th century, I shaded my eyes from the intense light that glared off the magnificent white stone buildings with their impressive carved doors—a fusion of Swahili, Arabic, Persian, Indian, and European architecture. There were no motorized vehicles, only donkeys and camels. The spell of soft white sand and clear blue water was interrupted only by the smell of donkey and camel dung.

When it came time for them to catch their flight back home to Durban, Malcie and I were crying, not knowing when we would see each other again. I boarded a flight to Dar es Salaam and waited for my flight home. It was a twelve-hour layover at the Dar airport and I sat on a metal folding chair for most of it.

During those twelve hours, I revisited my memories: the animals, the friends, the mountain, the smells and sounds of Africa, my brother and nephew, and how we had come together to take care of Mummy's wishes. I would say goodbye to a life that shaped me and for which I could finally express my gratitude.

# 15

# Retirement's Ups and Downs

*I do not regret one moment of my life.*

—Lillie Langtree

Tom retired in 1997 at fifty-six. I had encouraged him to retire early as he had worked so hard during his career, with long days and a great deal of travel overseas, sometimes for two or three weeks at a time. My friends could not imagine why I encouraged him to retire, but we had had very little time together.

In spite of all our exciting projects, as Tom's retirement approached, I did get a feeling of panic, wondering what I was going to do for myself, having been a corporate wife and mother for so many years. I had hoped to find something I would enjoy doing.

I was at Lake Tahoe on my own with our yellow Labrador, Floie, during a very bad winter that produced eleven feet of snow. Tom was traveling around the world saying his goodbyes to colleagues. For me, the days were long and lonely. I went to a gallery in Kings Beach and asked for a paint-by-numbers book. The owner, Lola, was delightful and she encouraged me to take some art lessons, which I did. I would stay up until 1:00 A.M. painting with the music turned up loud. That was my introduction to painting—and I loved it.

Two years later we were visiting friends in Jackson Hole, Wyoming. An artist I admired there sculpted whimsical wildlife. I visited her gallery with a close friend and left with a piece of clay the size of a golf ball. As I manipulated it, it spoke to me. I mentioned to Tom that I was going to take a sculpting class. Tom thought I should not mix mediums and stick to painting. Needless to say, I didn't listen and took sculpting lessons.

Now I sculpt wildlife, which gives me so much pleasure. I feel I have a real relationship with my subjects. I feel their hearts beating, their wet noses, their feathers and fur. I feel like the clay is alive. I have been most fortunate, as I have had many commissions. Some of my bronzes, in addition to being in the United States, have gone to collectors in Tasmania, Australia, England, New Zealand, Switzerland, and yachts that sail around the world.

Three years before Tom's retirement, we started to think about how we wanted to spend our future time together.

In 1995, we were invited to fly to San Jose del Cabo, Mexico, to look at a potential real estate development project with Don Koll, who owned the Palmilla Hotel and many other properties in Cabo.

I had no interest in going, because back in 1969, one of the trips we had taken, courtesy of my discount airline passes, was to Cabo San Lucas, twenty miles west of San Jose. At that time, Cabo was totally undeveloped. I disliked the place and vowed never to return.

After days of coercion by Tom, I was finally persuaded to join him and some friends at the Koll's lovely beachfront home next to the Palmilla Hotel. On the second day, the men went to check out the investment opportunity and the ladies were given a car and driver with Don's assistant to show us the environs and take us shopping.

At dinner that night, I told Tom there was something I wanted him to see before we left, as I would like to buy it. Tom's immediate reaction was "What piece of art or jewelry do you want to show me?"

The next day we drove to Palmilla Caleta to look at a piece of property, down the beach from Don's home. There, I announced to Tom that we should buy the lot.

"Forty-eight hours ago, you told me how much you disliked Los Cabos and had no desire to come here again," Tom said. "Now you want to buy a piece of property and build a home!"

Thus began retirement project Number One and the beginning of Casa Paulina, a beautiful traditional Spanish-style home on the oceanfront. We bought the land in 1995 and in 1997, shortly after Tom retired, we drove from Ross, California (where we kept our home) to our Mexico home and delivered our car.

So I, too, had found a remote property, just as Tom had done in New Zealand in 1972. We are most relaxed at Casa Paulina.

We loved Napa Valley and after buying the Mexico property, we also looked at wineries in Sonoma County. In 1996 and 1997, we lost out on several attempts to acquire property in Napa, with and without wineries. This led us to our commitment to build an upscale lodge on our property in New Zealand. Construction commenced in June 1998 and Blanket Bay opened in December 1999, in one of the world's most magical settings, combining lake, alps, glaciers, rivers and farming country. The lodge, Blanket Bay, was named one of the first Small Luxury Hotels of the World in New Zealand.

Tom's work life, now centered in New Zealand, includes Blanket Bay and the surrounding 10,000 acres of Wyuna Station, ownership interests in a winery and vineyards, and raising sheep, cattle and deer for venison. We may have failed in Napa, but we succeeded in New Zealand!

## The New Century

The new century has had its ups and downs, though we prefer to dwell on the ups. In September of 2000, Tom was told he had breast cancer and three days later underwent a mastectomy. He had four months of chemotherapy and three months of radiation. It was a stressful time, of course, and hard on Tom, who never complained and was strong through the whole ordeal. He was always positive for my benefit. Ultimately, we moved forward.

A high point was Gregory and Virginia's wedding on December 31 at the Four Seasons in Santa Barbara, a magical experience. Gregory and Virginia have given us three darling grandchildren, Luke, Logan and Lucy.

In 2009, Scott and Christine were married at our home in San Jose del Cabo, Mexico, on our beach as the sun was setting. This was also a magical evening, and they have given us our dear grandson, James.

Having had two sons, we finally got the daughters we didn't have—and today have two lovely daughters-in-law, Virginia and Christine, and two darling grand-daughters, in addition to our grandsons.

We feel so fortunate to have our children living within twenty minutes of our home in Ross.

## Reflections

Today, life is amazing. My days, months and years are spent with Tom, precious sons and daughters-in-law, and being a loving grandmother to all my grand-children. I enjoy travels with Tom to our lodge in New

Zealand, our homes in Lake Tahoe and Mexico, and of course, time spent in Ross. I find moments of calm combined with exhilaration in my artwork—I love to sculpt and cast wildlife in bronze. This is a relatively newfound hobby but one I cherish. I am hands-on involved in the Tusher African exhibit at the California Academy of Sciences, where Tom and I have had an opportunity to give back to the community and share all that is good about the Africa I love.

Life has surprising twists and turns. There I was at fourteen, on the slopes of Mt. Kilimanjaro, dreaming of visiting the Caribbean and the Pacific—and at twenty-nine, I had already lived in both places. To me this is the difference between fate and destiny—fate is what happens to you, destiny is what you help make happen.

Made in the USA
Coppell, TX
13 August 2022

81414111R00079